T0198956

An Analysis of

Henry Kissinger's

World Order
Reflections on the Character of
Nations and the Course of History

Bryan R. Gibson

Published by Macat International Ltd
24:13 Coda Centre, 189 Munster Road, London SW6 6AW.

Distributed exclusively by Routledge
2 Park Square, Milton Park, Abingdon, Oxon OX14 4RN
711 Third Avenue, New York, NY 10017, USA

Routledge is an imprint of the Taylor & Francis Group, an informa business

www.macat.com
info@macat.com

Cataloguing in Publication Data
A catalogue record for this book is available from the British Library.
Library of Congress Cataloguing-in-Publication Data is available upon request.
Cover illustration: Kim Thompson

ISBN 978-1-912303-34-2 (hardback)
ISBN 978-1-912128-83-9 (paperback)
ISBN 978-1-912282-22-7 (e-book)

CONTENTS

THE MACAT LIBRARY

The Macat Library is a series of unique academic explorations of seminal works in the humanities and social sciences – books and papers that have had a significant and widely recognised impact on their disciplines. It has been created to serve as much more than just a summary of what lies between the covers of a great book. It illuminates and explores the influences on, ideas of, and impact of that book. Our goal is to offer a learning resource that encourages critical thinking and fosters a better, deeper understanding of important ideas.

Each publication is divided into three Sections: Influences, Ideas, and Impact. Each Section has four Modules. These explore every important facet of the work, and the responses to it.

This Section-Module structure makes a Macat Library book easy to use, but it has another important feature. Because each Macat book is written to the same format, it is possible (and encouraged!) to cross-reference multiple Macat books along the same lines of inquiry or research. This allows the reader to open up interesting interdisciplinary pathways.

To further aid your reading, lists of glossary terms and people mentioned are included at the end of this book (these are indicated by an asterisk [*] throughout) – as well as a list of works cited.

Macat has worked with the University of Cambridge to identify the elements of critical thinking and understand the ways in which six different skills combine to enable effective thinking. Three allow us to fully understand a problem; three more give us the tools to solve it. Together, these six skills make up the **PACIER** model of critical thinking. They are:

ANALYSIS – understanding how an argument is built
EVALUATION – exploring the strengths and weaknesses of an argument
INTERPRETATION – understanding issues of meaning

CREATIVE THINKING – coming up with new ideas and fresh connections
PROBLEM-SOLVING – producing strong solutions
REASONING – creating strong arguments

To find out more, visit **WWW.MACAT.COM.**

CRITICAL THINKING AND *WORLD ORDER*

Primary critical thinking skill: INTERPRETATION
Secondary critical thinking skill: REASONING

Henry Kissinger's 2014 book *World Order: Reflections on the Character of Nations and the Course of History* not only offers a summary of thinking developed throughout a long and highly influential career—it is also an intervention in international relations theory by one of the most famous statesmen of the twentieth century. Kissinger initially trained as a university professor before becoming Secretary of State to President Richard Nixon in 1973 – a position in which he both won the Nobel Peace Prize and was accused of war crimes by protesters against American military actions in Vietnam. While a controversial figure, Kissinger is widely agreed to have a unique level of practical and theoretical expertise in politics and international relations – and *World Order* is the culmination of a lifetime's experience of work in those fields.

The product of a master of the critical thinking skill of interpretation, *World Order* takes on the challenge of defining the worldviews at play in global politics today. Clarifying precisely what is meant by the different notions of 'order' imagined by nations across the world, as Kissinger does, highlights the challenges of world politics, and sharpens the focus on efforts to make surmounting these divisions possible. While Kissinger's own reputation will likely remain equivocal, there is no doubting the interpretative skills he displays in this engaging and illuminating text.

ABOUT THE AUTHOR OF THE ORIGINAL WORK

Born in southern Germany in 1923, **Henry Kissinger** fled with his Jewish family to the United States to escape the Nazis in 1938. He began his career in academia, but soon turned to politics. As national security advisor to US presidents Nixon and Ford (1969–75), and as secretary of state (1973–77), Kissinger was responsible for American foreign policy during a critical period in the country's history. He won the Nobel Peace Prize for helping bring about the American withdrawal from Vietnam in 1973. Since leaving public office in 1977, Kissinger has continued to advise on foreign policy.

ABOUT THE AUTHOR OF THE ANALYSIS

Dr Bryan Gibson holds a PhD in International History from the London School of Economics (LSE) and was a post-doctoral research fellow at the LSE's Centre for Diplomacy and Strategy and an instructor on Middle Eastern politics at both the LSE's Department of International History and the University of East Anglia's Department of Political, Social and International Studies (PSI).
He is currently on the faculty of Johns Hopkins University and is the author of *Sold Out? US Foreign Policy, Iraq, the Kurds and the Cold War* (Palgrave Macmillan, 2015).

ABOUT MACAT

GREAT WORKS FOR CRITICAL THINKING

Macat is focused on making the ideas of the world's great thinkers accessible and comprehensible to everybody, everywhere, in ways that promote the development of enhanced critical thinking skills.

It works with leading academics from the world's top universities to produce new analyses that focus on the ideas and the impact of the most influential works ever written across a wide variety of academic disciplines. Each of the works that sit at the heart of its growing library is an enduring example of great thinking. But by setting them in context – and looking at the influences that shaped their authors, as well as the responses they provoked – Macat encourages readers to look at these classics and game-changers with fresh eyes. Readers learn to think, engage and challenge their ideas, rather than simply accepting them.

'Macat offers an amazing first-of-its-kind tool for interdisciplinary learning and research. Its focus on works that transformed their disciplines and its rigorous approach, drawing on the world's leading experts and educational institutions, opens up a world-class education to anyone.'

Andreas Schleicher
Director for Education and Skills, Organisation for Economic Co-operation and Development

'Macat is taking on some of the major challenges in university education ... They have drawn together a strong team of active academics who are producing teaching materials that are novel in the breadth of their approach.'

Prof Lord Broers,
former Vice-Chancellor of the University of Cambridge

'The Macat vision is exceptionally exciting. It focuses upon new modes of learning which analyse and explain seminal texts which have profoundly influenced world thinking and so social and economic development. It promotes the kind of critical thinking which is essential for any society and economy. This is the learning of the future.'

Rt Hon Charles Clarke, former UK Secretary of State for Education

'The Macat analyses provide immediate access to the critical conversation surrounding the books that have shaped their respective discipline, which will make them an invaluable resource to all of those, students and teachers, working in the field.'

Professor William Tronzo, University of California at San Diego

WAYS IN TO THE TEXT

KEY POINTS

- Henry Kissinger (b. 1923) is a German-born American scholar, diplomat, and Nobel Peace Prize-winning* statesman.

- His book *World Order* (2014) offers a historical account of how what he terms "world order"*—a stable system of relations between states—has been understood in different parts of the world.

- The book examines the continuing debate, heightened since the fall of the communist* Soviet Union* in 1991, between "realists,"* who contend that the risk of instability and conflict remains high, and "liberal internationalists,"* who believe that cooperation between nations will grow if policies that promote international structures fostering a liberal* world order are pursued.

Who is Henry Kissinger?

Heinz Alfred "Henry" Kissinger is one of the best-known and most controversial statesmen of the twentieth century. He was United States national security advisor* (1969–75) and secretary of state* (1973–77) during the presidencies of Richard Nixon* and Gerald Ford.*[1] During this time, he was accused of being complicit in human rights violations.

Kissinger was born in 1923 in the Bavarian town of Fürth in southern Germany.[2] His family was prosperous and Jewish. With the rise of the Nazis* in 1933, and the persecution of Germany's Jews that Nazism brought with it, his family were increasingly threatened. In 1938 the Kissinger family fled for America, as did many German Jews. There Kissinger adopted "Henry," the anglicized version of his name, although he continued to speak with a heavy German accent. After the United States joined World War II* in 1941, Kissinger was drafted into the US army and became a naturalized American citizen. His fluent German and knowledge of Nazi Germany saw him work in counterintelligence (efforts to prevent spying), at which he excelled.

After the war, Kissinger enrolled at Harvard University, where he studied politics and philosophy. He earned his Bachelor of Arts in 1950, his Master of Arts in 1951, and his Doctor of Philosophy in 1954. Kissinger was awarded a faculty position at Harvard, emerging as a vocal critic of American foreign policy. This brought him to the attention of senior members of the right-wing Republican Party* such as presidential candidate Nelson Rockefeller.* In 1969, President Richard Nixon asked Kissinger to serve as his national security advisor; for the next five years they would work to reshape the realm of international politics.

Kissinger's skilled diplomacy earned him the Nobel Peace Prize for his role in bringing about the American withdrawal from the Vietnam War* in 1973—a brutal Cold War* proxy war (that is, a war begun by two major powers that do not participate in the conflict) fought between American-backed South Vietnamese forces and the communist North Vietnamese forces backed by the Soviet Union and China. Since leaving public office in 1977, Kissinger has continued to advise successive US governments on foreign policy.

What Does *World Order* Say?

World Order: Reflections on the Character of Nations and the Course of History offers an analysis of the history of one of the more challenging questions facing humanity: What is "world order"—roughly, a stable system of international relations—and how can we bring about a universally acceptable form of this international system?

To answer this question, Kissinger analyzes four principal forms of world order:

- The European "Westphalian" system,* founded on notions of sovereignty* (the right to govern a specific territory), legitimacy* (lawfulness), balance of power* (balance of military and political power between the states that constitute the international order), and national interests* (things a nation believes are vital to its political, military, economic, or diplomatic reputation and comfort, or to its survival).
- The universalist Islamic order* (an order founded on notions of the supremacy of the Islamic faith)
- The Sino-centric* Chinese order (according to which China is at the center of the civilized world)
- The American order, which is premised on the concepts of freedom, justice, and representative democracy.

He also addresses the three secondary conceptions of world order that developed in Japan, India, and Persia (modern-day Iran). As Kissinger points out, the Japanese and Indian conceptions of world orders developed separately from the Chinese order, largely due to their geographic isolation from China—Japan is an island nation and India is separated from China by the Himalayan mountain range. Similarly, the Persian conception of world order developed separately due to its geographic position at the crossroads of several civilizations: the Asian, European, Indian, and Islamic. Even though Persia adopted Islam as a national religion, its ancient heritage and its decision to subscribe to a minority sect of Islam—Shi'ism*—left it with a distinctly different conception of world order.

Today, the dominant conception of world order is the Westphalian system that developed in the seventeenth century after the brutalities of the Thirty Years' War* (a European conflict between the political body known as the Holy Roman Empire* and several Germanic states that escalated into most of Europe). At the end of the war, with much of continental Europe suffering the consequences of a serious conflict, European statesmen developed the concepts of sovereignty, legitimacy, balance of power, and national interests as a means of resolving future differences. On the signing of the treaty known as the Peace of Westphalia* in 1648, which brought an end to the war, the signatories agreed to respect the legitimacy of the leaders of each state and not to interfere with their internal affairs. They established diplomatic representatives in each other's countries to resolve disputes peacefully. More importantly, in the event that one state became too powerful, it was agreed in principle that the others would form an alliance to restore equilibrium in the system, which came to be known as a "balance of power."

After centuries of evolution and inevitable modification, the Westphalian system still generally serves as the scaffolding for modern international relations. However, as Kissinger shows in *World Order*, it is no longer universally and easily accepted; the current international system can be understood as being a relic of the colonial* era—that is, a system forced on colonial subjects by European "masters." Today, challenges come from the alternative conceptions of world order, whether the Chinese, the Islamic, or the American.

For example, the Chinese system, being Sino-centric, views China as the center of the world and, as an emerging superpower, China will inevitably want to increasingly impose itself on the wider world. According to the universalist Islamic conception of world order, those who subscribe to Islam are part of the *dar al-Islam**—the "house of

Islam"; those who do not subscribe to Islam belong to *dar al-harb*,* the "realm of war," and are cast as outsiders, "others,"* who need either to be converted or face the wrath of God. The most extreme version of this conception is preached by militant groups such as the Islamic State of Iraq and Syria (ISIS),* its allies in al-Qaeda,* and its Nigerian affiliate, Boko Haram.*

Why Does *World Order* Matter?

World Order is a significant contribution to an ongoing debate among scholars of American foreign policy and of international relations about how a new world order can be forged. The debate is very largely a product of the end of the Cold War of 1947–91. Apart from the military threat it presented, the Cold War was an ideological standoff between the two most obvious beneficiaries of World War II, the United States and the Soviet Union. While both emerged as superpowers after 1945, they were entirely opposed ideologically.

Both wanted to impose their ideologies on the world; the Soviet Union was a communist power (that is, property was held in common ownership and labor organized for common benefit), but governed on authoritarian* principles—that is, governmental authority intruded into the citizen's life at the expense of liberty. The United States, which saw itself as the leader of what was called the "free world" (denoting the non-communist countries of the world) stood for capitalism* (an economic system in which industry and trade are held in private hands) and democracy. It would seem that American values prevailed when, essentially bankrupt, the Soviet Union collapsed in 1991. Yet the Cold War had provided a certain degree of stability to the Eastern Bloc;* the inevitable question after 1991 was what, if anything, could replace it.

In the United States, which then emerged as the sole superpower,* scholars were divided into two main groups. "Realists," such as the international relations scholars John Mearsheimer* and Stephen

Walt,* believed that very little would change with the collapse of the Soviet Union because the nature of international politics had not been fundamentally altered: states would continue to operate on the basis of how they could best exercise their own power, assessing and reacting to events in terms of their national interests. According to this analysis, it was unlikely that the rate of interstate conflict would decrease.

The second group, "liberal internationalists," such as the international relations scholars Anne-Marie Slaughter,* Robert Keohane,* and Joseph Nye, Jr.,* believed that the post-Cold War era would usher in a new age of international cooperation and that the power politics of the great powers (Great Britain, France, Germany, Russia, China, and the United States) would be consigned to the past. This group was more optimistic, believing that interstate conflict would be reduced if international bodies such as the United Nations* were strengthened. It was not a view that necessarily argued against military intervention, for example if intervention was used in instances where governments were unable—or unwilling— to protect their citizens.

Even though Kissinger declares himself a realist, the views expressed in *World Order* suggest that he tends to straddle these two positions. On the one hand, his outlook is realist in that he believes that the projection of power and securing legitimacy—roughly, a legal basis to exist—are central to the conduct of foreign relations, and that foreign interventions should be decided on the basis of a nation's national interests rather than by theoretical notions of morality. On the other, he also holds the liberal position that international institutions need to be strengthened in order to facilitate cooperation and prevent conflict.

NOTES

1 Christopher Hitchens, *The Trial of Henry Kissinger* (London: Verso, 2001).

2 Robert Dallek, *Nixon and Kissinger: Partners in Power* (London: HarperCollins, 2007), 34.

MODULE 1
THE AUTHOR AND THE HISTORICAL CONTEXT

KEY POINTS

- *World Order* is a significant contribution to the long-standing debate about how to create a new world order.*

- Henry Kissinger is a Nobel Prize-winning* diplomat, scholar, and statesman of international stature. He served as US secretary of state*—the highest diplomatic position in the US government—between 1973 and 1977.

- The inability to bring about a stable world order following the end of the Cold War* (a decades-long nuclear standoff between the Soviet Union* and the United States, and nations aligned to each, which ended with the collapse of the Soviet Union in 1991) convinced Kissinger that writing this book was necessary.

Why Read This Text?

Henry Kissinger's *World Order: Reflections on the Character of Nations and the Course of History* provides an important analysis of one of the greatest challenges mankind has faced: how to bring about a universally accepted world order—a structure of international relations, balances of power, and governance on which citizens of all nations can agree. One of the Western world's most respected statesmen and foreign-policy analysts, Kissinger is uniquely positioned to explore this key question. He shows that there are currently four major conceptualizations of world order:

- The European Westphalian* system
- The universal Islamic order*
- The Chinese Sino-centric order*
- The American order.

> 66 If I had to choose between justice and disorder, on the one hand, and injustice and order, on the other, I would always choose the latter. 99
>
> Henry Kissinger, in Robert Dallek, *Nixon and Kissinger*

Of these, the dominant system today is the Westphalian system first developed in the seventeenth century, if subsequently much changed—an order founded on notions of sovereignty,* legitimacy,* balance of power,* and national interests.* But as Kissinger makes plain in *World Order*, it is a system under attack from all directions. The path toward a viable new world order remains uncertain.

For those interested in the concept of world order, or in international politics more generally, *World Order* offers a comprehensive overview of world history and provides insights into the historical development of key sources of conflict and stability. This is particularly important today, now that the challenges that typically confronted states during the twentieth century—not just wars, but the Cold War too—are significantly altered. New threats have emerged from entities that are not states themselves in any conventional sense, most obviously the militant religious group known as the Islamic State of Iraq and Syria* (ISIS). Nature, likewise, presents its own threats in the form of potentially devastating pandemics, such as the outbreak of the infectious disease Ebola* that killed almost 25,000 people in West Africa in 2014.[1] As the challenges facing states become increasingly global, a new world order is needed ever more urgently.[2]

Author's Life

Heinz Alfred Kissinger was born on May 27, 1923 in the small Bavarian town of Fürth, in what was known as Weimar* Germany, the fragile republic set up in the disastrous aftermath of World War I.* His family was middle-class and Jewish; his mother, Paula Stern, came from a well-to-do family, and his father, Louis, was a schoolmaster at a state school. The Kissingers enjoyed considerable status in the town. Heinz Kissinger has a younger brother, Walter.[3]

Kissinger's adolescent years were increasingly difficult. The rise to power of Adolf Hitler* and the Nazi Party* he led in 1933 made Germany not merely an unpleasant but an actively dangerous place for an intellectually curious young Jewish boy.[4] In August 1938, Heinz and his family fled from Germany to America, where they had relatives. Though he shed his German name "Heinz" in favor of "Henry," his obvious German accent remained.

In 1943, Kissinger joined the army to fight in World War II.* He was sent to France, then to Germany, where he played an active role in the denazification of Germany after the end of the war in 1945. It was here that he found his first calling. His intelligence, fluent German, and firsthand knowledge of Nazi Germany made him an obvious asset.

After the war, Kissinger enrolled at Harvard, studying 16 hours a day and earning the highest honors. It was at Harvard, in 1949, that he married Ann Fleischer. They had two children, eventually divorcing in 1964. After his BA degree, Kissinger went on to earn his MA in 1951 and his PhD in 1954.

Having secured a tenured position at Harvard, Kissinger published a scathing series of articles attacking US foreign policy that caught the attention of the businessman Nelson Rockefeller,* then a presidential candidate, who enrolled Kissinger in his campaign as an advisor. After Rockefeller failed to win the Republican* nomination for the 1968 election, Richard Nixon,* who won the nomination (and the election), hired Kissinger as his national security advisor.* In 1973, Nixon appointed him secretary of state. Since leaving public life in 1977, Kissinger has remained a central figure in debates about the conduct of US foreign policy.

Author's Background

The Cold War had a profound impact on Kissinger's intellectual life. This ideological and geostrategic* conflict between the United States and Soviet Union began just as he started his education at Harvard (in a geostrategic conflict, politics and international relations are influenced by geography and by military and political strategy). Always alert to the past, Kissinger's PhD thesis "Peace, Legitimacy, and the Equilibrium (A Study of the Statesmanship of Castlereagh* and Metternich*)" focused on the role of statesmen in the Congress of Vienna,* the convention that forged a new European order after the defeat of Napoleon Bonaparte* in 1815.

Between 1955 and 1961, Kissinger published a dozen articles that criticized the conventional wisdom of foreign-policy making, garnering him national attention as a leading foreign-policy critic. In 1955, he published an article in the journal *Foreign Affairs* that attacked the administration of President Eisenhower* for pursuing a policy of massive nuclear retaliation—or mutually assured destruction*—in order to avoid war with the Soviet Union, and he advocated a strategy of fighting limited wars* to counter the expansion of the Soviet Union's influence. When this article was published in book form as *Nuclear Weapons and Foreign Policy* in 1957, it was an instant bestseller and Kissinger became a household name.

Today, Kissinger is best known for his role in the administration of President Nixon, who was forced to resign after disgracing himself in a political scandal, and his successor Gerald Ford.* In this time, Kissinger put his knowledge of foreign policy into practice, which led to an unmatched series of foreign-policy successes. In an 18-month period during 1972–3, Kissinger helped bring about "the end of the Vietnam War,* an opening to China, a summit with the Soviet Union even while escalating the military effort in response to a North Vietnamese offensive, the switch of Egypt from a Soviet ally to close cooperation with the United States, two disengagement agreements in the Middle East … and the start of the European Security Conference, whose outcome over the long term severely weakened Soviet control of Eastern Europe."[5]

NOTES

1 Centers for Disease Control and Prevention, "2014 Ebola Outbreak in West Africa – Case Counts," accessed November 18, 2015, http://www.cdc.gov/vhf/ebola/outbreaks/2014-west-africa/case-counts.html.

2 Wolfgang Ischinger, "The World According to Kissinger: How to Defend Global Order," *Foreign Affairs* (March/April 2015), accessed October 1, 2015, https://www.foreignaffairs.com/reviews/2015-03-01/world-according-kissinger.

3 Robert Dallek, *Nixon and Kissinger* (London: HarperCollins, 2007), 34.

4 Dallek, *Nixon and Kissinger*, 34.

5 Henry Kissinger, *World Order* (New York: Penguin, 2015), 307–8.

MODULE 2
ACADEMIC CONTEXT

KEY POINTS

- *World Order* is relevant to two fields of study: diplomatic history, which focuses on the history of diplomatic relations, and international relations, which focuses on relations between states and nongovernmental organizations.

- Theories of international relations are broken down into two camps: realist* and liberal internationalist.* Realists believe that states resort to aggression when their national interests are threatened, and that conflict is a constant of international politics. Liberals believe that in the absence of a dominant power (known as a hegemon),* states will tend to cooperate and that such cooperation is the norm of international politics.

- Henry Kissinger is a realist, a point made plain by the way he conducted foreign relations during his time at the White House.

The Work in its Context

Henry Kissinger's *World Order: Reflections on the Character of Nations and the Course of History* fits within two closely related academic disciplines: diplomatic history and international relations. While Kissinger is a famed practitioner of foreign policy, he is actually a diplomatic historian by trade, whose research focused on the conduct of foreign relations.

Diplomatic historians use techniques such as archival research, memoirs, oral history, and document analysis, to develop a historical understanding of relations between states. Today, as governments make an increasing number of documents available to researchers, it

> **❝ I want you to meet this fellow Henry Kissinger, who is a combination of [Immanuel] Kant and [Benedict de] Spinoza. ❞**
>
> William Y. Elliott, in Robert Dallek, *Nixon and Kissinger*

is a field that has grown in popularity, both as an academic discipline and commercially, with major publishers putting out hugely successful works that deal with diplomacy. Kissinger's *World Order* is a prime example.

International relations is more a subdiscipline of politics. Its primary focus is the way in which countries and nongovernmental bodies, such as international organizations like the World Bank* (an organization founded to make loans to developing countries in return for economic reform), corporations (Microsoft, Apple, and Gap, for example), or terrorist groups (today, most obviously the Islamic State of Iraq and Syria),* interact with each other.

This field is by no means new. Scholars and philosophers, among them the Greek philosopher Aristotle,* the ancient Greek historian Thucydides,* and the fifteenth- and sixteenth-century political theorist Niccolò Machiavelli,* have long been interested in how groups of people (or nations) interact, and have developed sophisticated theories to help explain this. Such theories, like realism or idealism,* can play a major role in influencing how foreign-policy practitioners operate and what informs their decisions.

Overview of the Field

As a work of diplomatic history, Kissinger's *World Order* draws on the intellectual heritage of the nineteenth-century German historian Leopold von Ranke,* considered the father of the field. Ranke argued that only through archival research and the analysis of historical documents can any kind of objective truth—an accurate picture of historical events—be reached. For Ranke, historical events were best understood when developed into a chronological narrative, this being the optimum way to show the relationship between cause and effect. Both of these techniques are evident not just in *World Order* but in Kissinger's earlier historical works and in his memoirs, for which he often used documents produced during his time at the White House.

Kissinger's work also plays into a central debate among scholars of international relations, who are historically divided into two main factions: realists and idealists. Realists, such as Kissinger and presidents Theodore Roosevelt* and Richard Nixon,* see international politics as a matter of sovereign nations (a sovereign nation being an independent state that governs itself) balancing each other's power.* All three also believed in the projection of American power. As the international relations scholar Joseph Nye, Jr.* points out, to realists, "world order* is the product of a stable distribution of power among the major states."[1] Kissinger's association with realism stems from his time at Harvard, where Hans Morgenthau*—a classical realist*—convinced him that global politics was defined by power and a dispassionate calculation of a state's interests.[2]

The second school of thought is that of idealism (or liberalism). In American terms, it is associated primarily with President Woodrow Wilson,* president of the US between 1913 and 1921, and President Jimmy Carter,* in office between 1977 and 1981. Idealism bases its analysis on the assumption that nations and people are inherently good, and promotes values such as democracy and human rights. For idealist thinkers, cooperation among states should be encouraged, especially through international organizations such as the United Nations.*

Academic Influences

As a young scholar, two figures had a direct influence on Kissinger's intellectual growth and later career. The first was Fritz Kraemer,* a fellow German émigré and academic, whom Kissinger had met after joining the US army. According to Kissinger's biographer, "Kraemer helped arrange jobs for Henry that strengthened his self-confidence and added to feelings that he was not just a naturalized American but a German and ... a European with a keen feel for international affairs."[3] More importantly, it was Kraemer who convinced Kissinger to use the GI Bill* (legislation passed to provide benefits to former servicemen) to enroll at Harvard and to apply for a New York state scholarship.[4]

While at Harvard, Kissinger met his second principal influence, the historian William Y. Elliott,* a notable scholar of governance who had served as a presidential advisor for six US presidents and who agreed to serve as Kissinger's mentor. Elliott encouraged Kissinger's appetite for knowledge, demanding, for example, that he read 25 books on Immanuel Kant* and write a review of his works. Determined to impress, Kissinger completed the assignment in just three months, prompting Elliott to describe to his colleagues that he had "not had any students in the past five years ... who have had the depth and philosophical insight shown by Mr. Kissinger," whom he described as "a combination of Kant and [the famed Dutch philosopher] Spinoza."*[5] Through Elliott's encouragement, guidance, and support, Kissinger applied for and was accepted into Harvard's PhD program.

NOTES

1 Joseph S. Nye, Jr., "What New World Order?" *Foreign Affairs* (Spring 1992): 84–5, accessed December 7, 2015, https://www.foreignaffairs.com/articles/1992-03-01/what-new-world-order.

2 Hans Morgenthau, *Politics Among Nations: The Struggle for Power and Peace* (New York: Knopf, 1948).

3 Robert Dallek, *Nixon and Kissinger* (London: HarperCollins, 2007), 37–8.

4 Dallek, *Nixon and Kissinger*, 39.

5 Dallek, *Nixon and Kissinger*, 41.

MODULE 3
THE PROBLEM

KEY POINTS

- When *World Order* was published in 2014, the debate about the nature of world order* had subsided since a flurry of activity in the 1990s and early 2000s.

- In the 1990s, the realist* school of international relations contended that the new world order would be based on the projection of Western values of individualism and liberty, and the belief that disorder will probably exist on the fault lines of the world's major civilizations. For the liberal* school of international relations, a new world order could be achieved through the strengthening and reform of international institutions such as the United Nations.*

- *World Order* tends to straddle these debates, drawing on both realist and liberal views.

Core Question

The central question of Henry Kissinger's *World Order* is: What is world order and how is it viewed around the world? The idea of a new world order is not particularly new—and nor is it unique to Kissinger's work, directly reflecting a debate among scholars of international relations since the end of the Cold War* (particularly with respect to American foreign policy). After the final collapse of Europe's communist* states with the end of the Soviet Union* in 1991, the term became closely associated with the administration of President George H. W. Bush,* which declared its intention to renounce the unilateralism* (action taken by a single state without the agreement or support of other states) of the Cold War era in favor of multilateral* diplomacy and, if necessary, military action.

> **❝** This book grew out of a dinner conversation
> with Charles Hill ... a valued member of the [state
> department's] policy planning staff when I served as
> secretary of state a lifetime ago ... At the dinner, we
> concluded that the crisis in the concept of world order
> was the ultimate problem of our day. **❞**
>
> Henry Kissinger, *World Order: Reflections on the Character of Nations and the Course of History*

Following the collapse of the Berlin Wall* dividing communist East Germany and democratic West Germany and the consequent "victory" of Western liberal democracy (in which the government respects the liberty of individual citizens), the US political scientist Francis Fukuyama* sparked a contentious debate over the question of what a post-Cold War order would look like with his 1989 article "The End of History?," subsequently published as the book *The End of History and the Last Man* in 1992. Fukuyama believed that a new order would develop based on Western liberal and democratic traditions. Over the course of the next 25 years, numerous scholars of international relations have contributed to this debate. That said, no consensus emerged as to what shape the post-Cold War order might take, nor on what role the United States would have in shaping it.

The Participants

After the publication of Fukuyama's *The End of History and the Last Man*, several scholars developed competing views on what the post-Cold War order would look like. In 1992, the international relations scholar Joseph Nye, Jr.* published a response to Fukuyama in an article in the journal *Foreign Affairs* that asked "What New World Order?" For him, "rather than the end of history, the post-Cold War world is witnessing a return of history in the diversity of sources of international conflict."[1] The next year, the US political scientist Samuel P. Huntington* published a detailed response to Fukuyama in the article "The Clash of Civilizations?" and the subsequent book *The Clash of Civilizations and the Remaking of World Order* (1996). Huntington argued that "in the emerging [post-Cold War] world, Western belief in the universality of Western culture suffers three problems: it is false; it is immoral; and it is dangerous."[2] For Huntington, "the fundamental source of conflict in this new world will not be primarily ideological or primarily economic. The great divisions among humankind and the dominating source of conflict will be cultural. Nation states will remain the most powerful actors in world affairs, but the principal conflicts of global politics will occur between nations and groups of different civilizations."[3]

The Contemporary Debate

Fukuyama and Huntington's theses prompted a response from liberal international relations scholars, who believed that a just new world order depended on the strengthening of international institutions. In 1997, the international relations scholar Anne-Marie Slaughter* published the article "The Real New World Order," in which she argued that a new world order was emerging, but not in the form of supra-state (above-state) bodies such as the United Nations* or the World Bank,* as Kissinger would argue. Instead, Slaughter believed that this new world order was actually emerging at the sub-state (below-state) level where a complex and interconnected network of representatives from bodies such as courts, regulatory agencies, and nongovernmental bodies such as the World Wildlife Fund* and Greenpeace,* cooperate to deal with transnational issues such as crime, terrorism, environmental degradation, and international relations—a process she called "transgovernmentalism."[4] This process is driven by incredible advances in technology, above all the Internet.

In 2001, the professor of international relations John Mearsheimer*
entered the debate about the post-Cold War world order in his book
The Tragedy of Great Power Politics. In it, Mearsheimer developed his
concept of offensive realism.* This holds that the international system
is anarchical* (that is, ungoverned), the great powers are the main
actors in global politics, all states possess offensive capabilities, states can
never be certain of each other's intentions, survival is the primary
objective, and all states are rational actors (that is, they act according to
rational decisions). In short, Mearsheimer believed that the end of the
Cold War did not reduce the likelihood of continued rivalry between
the most powerful nations.[5]

In the aftermath of the terrorist attacks on the United States on
September 11, 2001 (9/11)* and the subsequent War on Terror*
(that is, American-led actions throughout the Middle East against
non-state organizations and the US-led wars in Afghanistan* and
Iraq),* the debate about a new world order floundered. However, in
the mid-2000s there was an intellectual backlash against the
unilateralism of the George W. Bush* administration (that is, its
propensity to act alone) and its efforts to use American leverage in
international institutions to promote its own narrow vision of a US-
led world order.[6] In particular, liberals were dismayed by the
appointment of two key architects of the failed Iraq War, John
Bolton* and Paul Wolfowitz* as, respectively, the US ambassador to
the United Nations and the president of the World Bank.

In response, in his book *The Parliament of Man: The Past, Present, and
Future of the United Nations* (2006), Paul Kennedy* called for the
strengthening of international institutions, especially the United
Nations. Similarly, in 2009 the scholars of government Stephen
Brooks* and William Wohlforth* argued that there were five steps
that the new administration of President Barack Obama* needed to
take to reform international institutions and to forge a new order:

- Play up the reciprocal benefits of proposed reforms
- Ensure the revised framework provides public benefits, such as stifling terrorism and stabilizing the global economy
- Link the proposed order to the current order
- Consider possible objections from other states and then act so as to minimize their legal force
- Persuade others that change is needed.[7]

NOTES

1   Joseph S. Nye, Jr., "What New World Order?" *Foreign Affairs* (Spring 1992): 84–5, accessed December 7, 2015, https://www.foreignaffairs.com/articles/1992-03-01/what-new-world-order.

2   Samuel P. Huntington, *The Clash of Civilizations and the Remaking of World Order* (London: Simon and Schuster, 2002), 310.

3   Samuel P. Huntington, "The Clash of Civilizations?" *Foreign Affairs* (Summer 1993): 22, accessed December 7, 2015, https://www.foreignaffairs.com/articles/united-states/1993-06-01/clash-civilizations.

4   Anne-Marie Slaughter, "The Real New World Order," *Foreign Affairs* (September/October 1997): 183–4, accessed December 7, 2015, https://www.foreignaffairs.com/articles/1997-09-01/real-new-world-order.

5   John J. Mearsheimer, *The Tragedy of Great Power Politics* (New York: W. W. Norton, 2001).

6   Daniel W. Drezner, "The New New World Order," *Foreign Affairs* (March/April 2007): 34–46, accessed December 7, 2015, https://www.foreignaffairs.com/articles/2007-03-01/new-new-world-order.

7   Stephen G. Brooks and William C. Wohlforth, "Reshaping the World Order," *Foreign Affairs* (March/April 2009): 59, accessed December 7, 2015, https://www.foreignaffairs.com/articles/2009-03-01/reshaping-world-order.

MODULE 4
THE AUTHOR'S CONTRIBUTION

KEY POINTS

* Henry Kissinger does not specifically state how to bring about a new world order.*

* He examines the different understandings of world order in different parts of the globe and how these evolved over time.

* Building on the ongoing debate between the realist* and the liberal* schools of international relations, Kissinger uses European, Islamic, Asian, and American history to show how each of these civilizations understands the concept of world order.

Author's Aims

Henry Kissinger's primary objective when writing *World Order* was to explain the various interpretations of the concept of world order, to explain how these developed, and to identify potential obstacles to achieving a universally accepted world order in the future. For him, the central problem is that "no truly global 'world order' has ever existed";[1] until comparatively recently, communication between the regions of the world was limited at best. As a result, different views about world order developed in different regions and in different civilizations: the European Westphalian* order, with its principles of sovereignty* and legitimacy;* the Islamic order,* founded on the notion of the supremacy of the Muslim faith;* the Sino-centric* Asian order, according to which China should automatically be considered the center of any world order; and the American order, informed by the principles of democracy and liberty; and two

> ❝ Our age is insistently, at times almost desperately, in pursuit of a concept of world order. Chaos threatens side by side with unprecedented interdependence: the spread of weapons of mass destruction, the disintegration of states, the impact of environmental depredations [ravages], the persistence of genocidal practices, and the spread of new technologies threatening to drive conflict beyond human control or comprehension. ❞
>
> Henry Kissinger, *World Order: Reflections on the Character of Nations and the Course of History*

secondary Asian ones—the Japanese and Indian—which developed due to their relative geographic isolation from China.

Today, however, civilizations that had previously been isolated are able to communicate instantaneously—which, for Kissinger, is both a good and a bad thing. On the one hand, these global interactions have allowed for the spread of new ideas that could eventually form the basis of the universal order that Kissinger so desires. On the other hand, some of these ideas—the Chinese and the Islamic above all—are inherently hostile to the prevailing Western vision of world order.

Though Kissinger identifies these different approaches to world order, he does not suggest a potential solution to the current impasse.

Approach

In order to achieve his objective, Kissinger adopts an approach that applies historical analysis in a regional manner. He starts with an examination of European history, specifically of how the Peace of Westphalia* (a series of peace treaties) that ended the Thirty Years' War* between the political body known as the Holy Roman Empire* and several other neighboring European states in 1648 contributed to the formulation of modern concepts such as sovereignty, balance of power,* and legitimacy. These are ideas that European colonial* powers—Britain, France, Portugal, Spain, and so on—subsequently adopted in their colonial empires (that is, in the territories that they claimed, governed, and exploited overseas). For this reason, the prevailing conception of world order throughout the globe is based on these Westphalian concepts, and enshrined in international institutions, most notably the United Nations.*

Simply because a Western view of world order prevails throughout the world, however, it does not mean that it is accepted universally. For this reason, Kissinger then examines Islamic, Asian (that is, Japanese and Indian), Chinese, and American conceptions of world order, which differ in many ways from that developed in Europe. In each of these instances, Kissinger uses historical analysis to show how these conceptions developed, often based on each region's historical experiences and interactions with threatening European powers. Even the American view of world order, which is technically a descendent of the Westphalian order, differs from its European cousins in that it is premised on freedom, justice, and democracy. These are concepts that Adolf Hitler* or Joseph Stalin*—both European leaders, both on the opposite extremes of the political spectrum—could hardly have accepted as legitimate even though each otherwise accepted, albeit to varying degrees, the core concepts of the Westphalian order.

Contribution in Context

It is important to bear in mind that *World Order* was written toward the end of Kissinger's illustrious career as an academic and statesman. As an academic, Kissinger's publications have consistently focused on issues that relate in one way or another to world order. For example, the first two chapters of *World Order* deal with the establishment of the Westphalian order and the conference known as the Congress of Vienna,* held in 1815 to decide a new European political order following the defeat of Napoleon Bonaparte,* the French emperor who had brought most of continental Europe under French domination. Discussions of both these topics appear in most of Kissinger's publications. Indeed both formed the basis of Kissinger's initial academic inquiry *A World Restored: Metternich, Castlereagh and the Problems of Peace, 1812–22* (1957), which analyzed the role diplomats at the Congress of Vienna played in establishing the Westphalian system as the basis of all international relations in the West. Kissinger again returned to these themes in his lengthy work on the history of diplomatic relations, *Diplomacy* (1994), which also provides an extended discussion of American foreign policy. In 2011, Kissinger published *On China*, which focuses on the history of Sino-American relations and puts forward recommendations on how the United States should approach the rise of the Chinese superpower.* In other words, Kissinger had previously written on more than half of the topics under discussion in *World Order*.

The originality of *World Order* comes not from the material that he draws on to construct his narrative, but from how he uses this information to show that conceptions of world order are not unique to the West.

NOTES

1   Henry Kissinger, *World Order* (New York: Penguin, 2015), 2.

MAIN IDEAS

KEY POINTS

- The main themes of *World Order* are world order,* power, and legitimacy,* themes used by Kissinger to examine the European, Islamic, Asian, and American conceptions of world order.

- Henry Kissinger argues that order needs to be cultivated through diplomacy, not imposed through military force.

- The tone of the book is deliberately accessible, intended to appeal to general readers as well as specialists. The book is far from drily academic.

Key Themes

The main themes of Henry Kissinger's *World Order* are evident in the book's title: world order itself, power, and legitimacy. *World Order* examines how historical experiences around the world have resulted in distinctly different conceptualizations—European, Islamic, Asian, and American—of these ideas.

The most dominant view of world order is that of the European concept, which stems from the Westphalian* order that was developed in the seventeenth century, following the end of Europe's Thirty Years' War (1618–48).* The Peace of Westphalia* of 1648, signed to bring the conflict to an end, introduced the concepts of balance of power* and sovereignty.*

The Islamic conception of world order* is universal, deriving its power and legitimacy from religion. This view holds that Islam is destined to expand over the realms of non-believers until the whole world is brought under a unitary system based on the teachings of the Prophet Muhammad.*[1]

> **❝** World order describes the concept held by a region
> or civilization about the nature of just arrangements and
> the distribution of power thought to be applicable to
> the entire world. An international order is the practical
> application of these concepts to a substantial part of
> the globe—large enough to affect the global balance
> of power. Regional orders involve the same principles
> applied to a defined geographic area. **❞**
>
> Henry Kissinger, *World Order: Reflections on the Character of Nations and the Course of History*

The Asian order centers on multiplicity,* with several competing visions of order developing in China, Japan, and India. China viewed itself as the center of a hierarchical and universal concept of order. As Kissinger observed, "Sovereignty in the European sense did not exist, because the emperor held sway over 'All Under Heaven.'"[2] However, Japan developed separately from China even if inevitably it was influenced by its much larger neighbor. In Japan legitimacy is vested in the emperor, who is considered divine—the "Son of Heaven." However, since World War II,* Japan has adopted a largely Westphalian conception of power and legitimacy. Similarly, India, with its cultural roots based in the religion of Hinduism* rather than Chinese Confucianism* called for a multipolar* world order—a world order led by several more or less equally powerful nations—based on mutual respect, nonaggression, noninterference, equality and mutual benefit, and peaceful coexistence.[3]

Finally, the American sense of world order is derived from the European, but modified to take into consideration the concepts of freedom, justice, and American exceptionalism* (the idea that the United States stands apart from other nations, largely due to an ideology based on freedom, justice, and representative democracy):"In the American view of world order, peace and balance would occur naturally, and ancient enmities would be set aside—once other nations were given the same principled say in their own governance."[4]

Exploring the Ideas

The European concept of world order developed in the seventeenth century, following an extended period of war throughout the continent. As Kissinger explains, the Westphalian system was reliant on "a system of independent states refraining from interference in each other's domestic affairs and checking each other's ambitions through a general equilibrium of power."[5] Each state is assigned sovereignty—or authority and capacity to rule—over a set geographical area and acknowledges the "domestic structures and religious vocations of its fellow states as realities and refrains from challenging their existence."[6] Finally, should one state grow stronger than the other states, these other states would group together in an alliance, their combined strength allowing them to restore the balance of power.

The Islamic order finds its roots in the massive expansion of Islam from its Arabian heartlands in the seventh century following the death in 632 C.E. of Muhammad. Within 100 years, Islamic armies had conquered vast swathes of territory, from the Strait of Gibraltar (the stretch of water between North Africa and southern Spain) in the west, to parts of the Indian subcontinent in the east. As Kissinger observed; "Islam was at once a religion, a multiethnic superstate, and a new world order."[7] To those who lived within these Islamic territories—called *dar al-Islam** or "house of Islam"—it was their duty to incorporate into the Islamic empire the non-Muslim people that lived in the lands beyond—*dar al-harb** or the "realm of war." The strategy to achieve this universal view of world order is known as *jihad** ("struggle"—although often misinterpreted to mean "holy war").

The Asian concept of world order is the oldest. Ever since its unification in 221 B.C.E., China has stood at the center of the Asian order. China viewed itself as "the sole sovereign government of the world"—that is, "all under heaven"—and its emperor as the "linchpin between the human and the divine" worlds.[8] "In this view," Kissinger notes, "world order reflected a universal hierarchy, not an equilibrium of competing sovereign states,"[9] and all other states were required to pay tribute. In other words, the Chinese emperor was the sole representative of God on earth, and all worldly states were under his dominion. This is a conception of world order that in effect has continued even under the communist* government that seized control in 1949 and despite the fact that the last Chinese emperor was forced to abdicate in 1912.

Finally, the American conception of world order eschews traditional Westphalian concepts of balance of power and hierarchy in favor of a universal concept of order based on the principles of democracy, justice, and freedom. Referencing "manifest destiny,"* the widely held nineteenth-century doctrine that the United States was destined to expand westward from the Atlantic to the Pacific oceans, Kissinger notes: "America has played a paradoxical role in world order: it expanded across a continent in the name of manifest destiny while abjuring any imperial designs; exerted a decisive influence on momentous events while disclaiming any motivation of national interest; and became a superpower* while disavowing any intention to conduct power politics." As a result, America's concept of world order is somewhat idealistic and based on the spread of values that "it believed all other peoples aspired to replicate."[10]

Language and Expression

World Order is a commercial work, intended for a wide audience, so it is written in an accessible style designed to appeal to general readers as much as to specialists and other experts. This does not mean that either the language or the ideas explored in the book are unsophisticated. However, in comparison to earlier works such as *Diplomacy*, published in 1994, which was specifically aimed at specialists, *World Order*, much like Kissinger's 2011 book *On China*, is deliberately targeted at a much wider readership.

Kissinger, who is in his nineties, acknowledges in the text that he has staff who conduct his research and type out his manuscripts, and he is open about the level of editorial scrutiny that the text was given by his mainstream commercial publisher, Penguin, who would necessarily want the book to reach the largest possible audience. He points out that numerous colleagues, scholars, fact-checkers, acquaintances, and friends had read through the manuscript and offered editorial advice.[11] Taken together, these factors help explain why *World Order* is written in a much clearer and more comprehensible style than many of his other works.

NOTES

1 Henry Kissinger, *World Order* (New York: Penguin, 2015), 5.

2 Kissinger, *World Order*, 4–5.

3 Kissinger, *World Order*, 205.

4 Kissinger, *World Order*, 6.

5 Kissinger, *World Order*, 3.

6 Kissinger, *World Order*, 3.

7 Kissinger, *World Order*, 99.

8 Kissinger, *World Order*, 213.

9 Kissinger, *World Order*, 213.

10 Kissinger, *World Order*, 234.

11 Kissinger, *World Order*, 375–7.

MODULE 6
SECONDARY IDEAS

KEY POINTS

- The key secondary ideas of *World Order* are balance of power* (or equilibrium), sovereignty* (the right to exercise authority), and national interests* (those things a state believes are vital to its political, military, economic, or diplomatic reputation or survival).

- Because Europe imposed the dominant international system on the world through colonialism* (the policy of seizing territories and governing them for the sake of economic and political gains), these Westphalian* concepts are central to understanding how international relations operate.

- Kissinger argues that the impact of technology is changing the emergence of a new world order.

Other Ideas

The secondary themes of Henry Kissinger's *World Order* are sovereignty, balance of power, and national interests—concepts key to Kissinger's main theme of a universal world order, which he believes has never truly existed. He also identifies key challenges that world leaders face when seeking to bring about a new world order.

The concept of sovereignty refers to the authority that a ruler, state, or nation holds to govern its citizens or those of another state, or to control a geographic territory. A key factor in determining sovereignty is recognition by other states of the authority of a ruler or government over a given territory.

An important concept in the conduct of foreign affairs is the balance of power or "power equilibrium." For example, from the

> ❝ Westphalian principles are ... the sole generally recognized basis of what exists as a world order. ❞
>
> Henry Kissinger, *World Order: Reflections on the Character of Nations and the Course of History*

perspective of the realist* school of international relations, if all nations in the world had exactly the same military capability, wars would be unlikely because no one state could defeat any other; there would be a balance of power. However, as the theory goes, should one state gain an advantage over the rest, the rest would band together to challenge the more powerful state and restore the balance.

Another key concept of *World Order* is that of national interests: the goals that a country seeks to achieve and that it believes are vital to its continued survival. For example, the economy of the United States is reliant on imported foreign oil. If a hostile entity, whether a nation or a terrorist group, controlled these sources of oil, it would have the potential to cripple the US economy. So it is in America's national interests both to prevent such a hostile entity from ever controlling its supply of oil and to build up its own oil industry to reduce its reliance on foreign sources of oil.

Kissinger points out that the traditional notion of a Westphalian state has been attacked, eroded, or dismantled in recent years. A second challenge is that the political and economic organizations of the world are at variance with each other: the economic system has become global but states have not. A final challenge is the absence of an effective mechanism for world powers to consult and cooperate on important issues.[1]

Exploring the Ideas

The Peace of Westphalia* is considered a major turning point in world history. Signed in 1648, a series of three separate treaties brought about an end to the exceptionally destructive Thirty Years' War* (1618–48). As Kissinger observed, the concept of sovereignty that emerged out of the peace involved the "right of each [nation] to choose its own domestic structure and religious orientation free from intervention."[2] Moreover, "If a state [accepts] these basic requirements, it could be recognized as an international citizen able to maintain its own culture, politics, religion, and internal policies, shielded by the international system from outside intervention."[3] This citizenship—and the recognition of citizenship—in the international community is the scaffolding of an international system built on the belief that a ruler or state has sovereignty over the territory they govern.

The peace imposed by the treaties of Westphalia in 1648 established a balance of power in Europe. As Kissinger explains: "Any international order … must sooner or later reach an equilibrium, or else it will be in a constant state of warfare." Therefore, to avoid this outcome European statesmen recognized that a balance of the military and economic power of states was a desirable outcome of foreign policy. Kissinger identifies two ways in which a balance of power can be challenged: firstly, if a secondary state tries to "enter the ranks of the major powers and sets off a series of compensating adjustments by the other powers until a new equilibrium is established"; secondly, if a major country builds up its strength to a point where it threatens the balance of power.[4] A good example of the first was the destabilization of the European balance of power following the unification of Germany* in 1871 and its subsequent alliance with Austria–Hungary in 1879. By 1907 this threat had prompted Britain, France, and Russia to form an alliance known as the Triple Éntente* to resist the combined forces of Germany and Austria–Hungary. The collective response of the Allies (chiefly Britain, the Soviet Union, and the United States) which led to the defeat of Nazi Germany* in World War II* is a good example of the second.

Finally, Kissinger believes that every government's job is to protect its national interests. He recognizes that the interests of one state are not always compatible with those of its allies or its enemies. He quotes the nineteenth-century British prime minister Lord Palmerston:* "We have no eternal allies, and we have no perpetual enemies. Our interests are eternal and perpetual, and those interests it is our duty to follow."[5] In other words, a government needs to do what is best to achieve its objectives whether through diplomacy, covert action, or war.

Overlooked

Because *World Order* was published in 2014, there has not been much of an opportunity for scholars to examine the ideas and themes Kissinger puts forward in great detail. This, of course, will change in time, particularly as world events continue to change the way we understand the concept of world order.

Perhaps the one area that might be overlooked by scholars in the years to come is Kissinger's chapter dealing with the relationship between technology and world order. This chapter appeared almost as an afterthought, having been developed out of a conversation Kissinger had with a colleague. And yet it is probably the most original of all the chapters in the text, because it shows how humanity has entered a new technologically driven age. As Kissinger explained, "[every] age has ... a set of beliefs that explains the universe. Science and technology are the governing concepts of our age."[6] Indeed, since World War II and the development of computers, science and technology have brought about the start of a new age that is driven primarily by technology: the cyber age (that is, the computer-driven-information age). Kissinger argues that this new age has the potential to bring about revolutionary changes to concepts of world order, both positive and negative. While most readers of the text will focus on Kissinger's examination of the different perspectives on world order, this is the one area that might be overlooked.

MODULE 7
ACHIEVEMENT

KEY POINTS

- Henry Kissinger was successful in showing how European, Islamic, Asian, and American conceptions of world order differ due to different historical experiences.

- The most important factor enabling the success of *World Order* is Kissinger's reputation and wide knowledge of world history.

- The only factor that arguably limits the success of the text is the seemingly partisan position that Kissinger adopts on controversial issues such as Iran's nuclear program.*

Assessing the Argument

There is little question that Henry Kissinger's *World Order: Reflections on the Character of Nations and the Course of History* was successful in achieving its objective. Organizing his chapters more or less along regional lines, Kissinger weaves centuries of history together in an easily digestible manner, showing how each region developed its own particular understanding of world order, sovereignty,* legitimacy,* and how to achieve a balance of power.* The text starts off with a discussion of these core concepts before offering an overview of world history, starting first with Europe and the development of the Westphalian* system.

The text next turns to an account of the origins of the Islamic order and a discussion of Iran's unusual place in the Middle East, as both an ancient nation (Persia) with a long history of interaction with Europe and as the largest Shi'a* Muslim state (the Shi'a are followers of one of the two major branches of Islam, the Sunni* being the

> ❝ If you think America is doing just fine, then skip ahead to the poetry reviews. If, however, you worry about a globe spinning out of control, then *World Order* is for you. It brings together history, geography, modern politics and no small amount of passion ... [This] is a *cri de coeur* from a famous skeptic, a warning to future generations from an old man steeped in the past. ❞
>
> John Micklethwait, "As the World Turns: Henry Kissinger's 'World Order,'" *New York Times*

other). From there, Kissinger analyzes the politically multipolar* nature of Asia, looking closely at the Japanese and Indian views of world order. He then turns to a detailed discussion of the Chinese conception of world order.

In the seventh and eighth chapters Kissinger combines historical analysis with a traditional narrative of American history, focusing on American presidents such as Theodore Roosevelt* and Woodrow Wilson* and their role in shaping the American conception of world order. He highlights, too, how the United States emerged as the sole superpower* after the end of the Cold War.* Finally, Kissinger offers a chapter on the role technology will play in the shaping of a future world order, focusing on how it has both transformed the way nations interact and created new dangers.

In reading *World Order* it is quite clear that Kissinger achieves his overall objective of showing that a truly global world order has never existed and that there are considerable challenges that will need to be overcome if there is ever to be a universal conception of world order.

Achievement in Context

World Order (2014) was published at a time of turmoil in international politics. Throughout 2014, geopolitical challenges to global order emerged around the world. In the Middle East, the Syrian civil war* had descended into chaos, as a three-way conflict emerged between the Syrian government, US- and Saudi-backed militants, and a radical Islamist group calling itself the Islamic State of Iraq and Syria* (ISIS), or simply the Islamic State. Quite unexpectedly, in June 2014 the Islamic State managed to seize and occupy large swathes of Syria and Iraq, including Iraq's second largest city, Mosul. In Asia, China began to flex its military and economic muscle, particularly over islands in the South China Sea. At the same time, the world's attention was fixed on the mysterious disappearance of Malaysia Airlines Flight 370;* to date, its disappearance has not been fully explained. In Eastern Europe tensions erupted following protests in Ukraine,* which toppled the Russian-backed government. During the chaos, Russia annexed the Crimean Peninsula (a territory on the northern coast of the Black Sea also known as Crimea) and civil war broke out. Further disruption was caused by the outbreak of the Ebola virus* in West Africa in March 2014, which resulted in the deaths of nearly 25,000 people.[1]

When *World Order* was published in September that year, the German diplomat Wolfgang Ischinger* noted in a review of the book that "to call *World Order* timely would be an understatement, for if there was one thing the world yearned for in 2014, it was order."[2] Another reviewer described the text as an "urgently written book" that serves as "a memorandum to future generations of policymakers that the next half-century will be no easier to manage than the most recent one."[3]

Limitations

It is a bit too early to tell whether or not *World Order* will have a major impact on the ongoing debate—both inside and outside academia—about how, if at all, a world order can be achieved. But it should be noted that, because the text consists of a broad exposition of world history, *World Order* does not face limitations of either its place or time; it could be argued that it will continue to be valuable in this regard for the foreseeable future, even if its references to events such as the emergence of ISIS and the Russian intervention in Ukraine are contemporary to 2014.

That the text is also distinctly pro–American, however, is scarcely a surprise given that Kissinger has spent his entire adult life as a champion and practitioner of American foreign policy. This is particularly the case in his chapter dealing with American–Iranian relations, where he suggests that Iran made rapid progress toward acquiring nuclear weapons during its negotiations with the five permanent members of the United Nations Security Council* (China, France, Russia, the UK, and the US) and Germany.[4] The claim is, however, conjecture, and unsubstantiated by facts: there is no evidence that Iran is seeking to build a nuclear bomb, nor that it has made progress toward acquiring nuclear weapons. There is also considerable evidence that shows that its nuclear capacity was significantly reduced during the negotiations.[5] And yet, Kissinger's historical account of the rise of Islam is both thoughtful and accurate, as are his chapters on Asia. Kissinger's pro–American bias, in other words, does not entirely diminish the work's usefulness.

NOTES

1   Wolfgang Ischinger, "The World According to Kissinger: How to Defend Global Order," *Foreign Affairs* (March/April 2014), accessed October 1, 2015, https://www.foreignaffairs.com/reviews/2015-03-01/world-according-kissinger.

2   Ischinger, "The World According to Kissinger."

3   Rana Mitter, "'World Order' by Henry Kissinger – review," *Guardian*, October 1, 2014, accessed October 15, 2015, http://www.theguardian.com/books/2014/oct/01/world-order-by-henry-kissinger-review-account.

4   Henry Kissinger, *World Order* (New York: Penguin, 2015), 159.

5   Arms Control Association, "Iran Nuclear Negotiations: Separating Myth from Reality," *Issue Briefs* 7, no. 2 (January 2015), accessed November 4, 2015, https://www.armscontrol.org/issue-briefs/2015-01-23/Iran-Nuclear-Negotiations-Separating-Myth-from-Reality.

MODULE 8
PLACE IN THE AUTHOR'S WORK

KEY POINTS

- Henry Kissinger's whole life has been spent studying and engaging in global politics. This theme is present throughout his entire body of work.

- *World Order* is the work of an elderly academic, diplomat, and statesman and therefore is the product of a depth of knowledge and years of experience practicing statecraft.

- *World Order* may be Kissinger's final publication.

Positioning

Henry Kissinger's *World Order: Reflections on the Character of Nations and the Course of History* comes at the end of a long and highly successful career as both an academic and a statesman. Between 1957 and 2015, he published 14 academic works and 3 memoirs, recounting his experiences in government as the national security advisor* and secretary of state* to presidents Richard Nixon* and Gerald Ford.* As a result, *World Order* is the work of a mature thinker who has spent much of his life pondering questions of power, the equilibrium in power between the nations of the international scene, and world order.

Kissinger has always been a staunch proponent of realpolitik,* the view that policy decisions should be driven by pragmatic, rather than by moral or ideological, considerations. This is evident not just in his writings, but also in the actions he took during his time in the White House. For example, in 1972, Kissinger and Nixon, both hardliners when it came to "fighting" the Cold War,* devised a strategy to increase American power at the expense of the Soviet Union.* Recognizing that Moscow's relations with Beijing had deteriorated,

> 66 Americans like the cowboy ... who rides all alone
> into the town, the village, with his horse and nothing
> else ... This amazing, romantic character suits me
> precisely because to be alone has always been part of
> my style or, if you like, my technique. 99
>
> Henry Kissinger, *White House Years*

they renewed diplomatic relations with communist* China, which, in turn, forced the Soviet Union to agree to a series of bilateral (two-way) agreements, during a period often referred to as détente* (a policy implemented by the United States between 1969 and 1979 to ease tension with the Soviet Union). This move was a singularly notable diplomatic coup, allowing the US to improve relations with both the Soviet Union and China while simultaneously extricating itself from the bloody Vietnam War.*

Integration

Within the context of Kissinger's broader body of work, *World Order* may very well be his last publication; at the age of 92, it is impressive that he is still publishing. It is plainly evident that a common thread weaves through his work: the study of power and order in international affairs.

His first book, *A World Restored* (1957), for example, an adaptation of his doctoral thesis, focuses on the establishment of a new balance of power in Europe at the Congress of Vienna* following the defeat of the French emperor Napoleon Bonaparte* in 1815. However, it was his next book, *Nuclear Weapons and Foreign Policy* (1957), that caught the attention of policy-makers and the public. In it, Kissinger fused political and military thinking with the doctrine of limited war* to establish himself as a leading foreign-policy critic, thereby propelling him toward a career as a diplomat and statesman.[1] Once again, the focus of Kissinger's work was how to create order at a time of great political, economic, and military uncertainty.

During the 1960s, Kissinger wrote several more books that cemented his position as a public academic figure, among them *The Necessity for Choice* (1961), which argued for a flexible response to Soviet aggression using conventional forces, *The Troubled Partnership* (1965), which reappraised the nature of America's relationship with its European allies, and, just prior to entering the White House, *American Foreign Policy: Three Essays* (1969), which lays out his views on the stresses affecting American foreign-policy making.

On leaving office, Kissinger published several memoirs about his time in office: *The White House Years* (1979), *Years of Upheaval* (1982), and, much later, *Years of Renewal* (1999). In the 1980s and 1990s, Kissinger mostly published collections of essays, statements, and declassified transcripts of his time in office. In 1994 he published a massive work, *Diplomacy*, which offered a grand account of diplomatic history over the centuries—perhaps his most significant contribution to the study of diplomacy to date.

In recent years, Kissinger has readdressed himself to academic concerns, with his *On China* (2011), analyzing Chinese history in terms of foreign policy, and *World Order* (2014). Both texts focus heavily on diplomatic history and the concept of world order.

Significance

Overall, Kissinger's contributions to the study of diplomatic history and foreign policy are significant. He has stood out as a strong proponent for an interest-based form of foreign policy driven by a realistic analysis of the facts of the situation, which need to be understood within their historical context.

World Order stands out as a perfect example of his outlook. In it, Kissinger offers his readers valuable insight into the development of the four great views of world order and explains how these groups differ. This, of course, requires a great deal of research along with knowledge and empathy. It is often difficult for those who are unfamiliar with the rest of the world or their histories to understand their point of view. In *World Order*, Kissinger conveys these views in a way that's easy to understand; for those who follow the events unfolding in the Middle East, for example, his chapter "Islamism and the Middle East" offers a sound description of how Islam emerged as a powerful force in the seventh century, while going into considerable depth about the origins of modern Islamic ideology. It is certainly not the antagonistic account that may have been expected.

NOTES

1   Hans Morgenthau, "Review: *Nuclear Weapons and Foreign Policy* by Henry A. Kissinger," *American Political Science Review* 52, no. 3 (September 1958): 842.

MODULE 9
THE FIRST RESPONSES

KEY POINTS

- *World Order* has been praised for its contribution to the debate over world order,* but criticized for Kissinger's failure to offer critical appraisals of living presidents such as George W. Bush* or Barack Obama.*

- Because the text was published in 2014, there has not yet been enough time for a debate to emerge in response to the text.

- The most important factor shaping the reception of *World Order* is Kissinger's controversial reputation, with those who dislike him writing negative reviews and those who agree with him writing positive ones.

Criticism

Because *World Order: Reflections on the Character of Nations and the Course of History* was written by a notably controversial figure in Henry Kissinger, it was bound to be reviewed by many of the major media outlets and by members of America's foreign-policy elite. Due to Kissinger's notoriety as a hard-nosed realist,* who has been accused of human-rights abuses in several countries due to decisions he made while in office,[1] there are plenty of people who dislike him on personal or ideological grounds. The majority of reviews, however, were quite positive. The former secretary of state Hillary Clinton,* for example, a politician who subscribes to a different political philosophy in the field of international relations, wrote that *World Order* "is vintage Kissinger, with his singular combination of breadth and acuity along with his knack for connecting headlines to trend lines."[2]

> ❝ [*World Order*] is a book that every member of Congress should be locked in a room with—and forced to read before taking the oath of office. ❞
>
> John Micklethwait, "As the World Turns: Henry Kissinger's 'World Order'," *New York Times*

Nevertheless, the most commonly cited critique of *World Order* stems from Kissinger's steadfast refusal to be critical of living presidents, particularly George W. Bush. In particular, reviews—such as the one in the *Economist*—took exception to his "sugaring his criticism of living statesmen with compliments that are, presumably, designed to spare the client's embarrassment."[3] For example, instead of offering justifiable criticism of the Bush administration's handling of the Iraq War,* Kissinger wrote: "I want to express here my continuing respect and personal affection for [Bush], who guided America with courage, dignity, and conviction in an unsteady time."[4] Referring to the former US president Woodrow Wilson,* known for his role in reconstructing Europe after World War I,* the journalist James Traub* shared the *Economist*'s concern, pointing out his disbelief that Kissinger would lavish "praise on the most reckless of Wilsonian [idealists]* of them all, George W. Bush."[5]

Responses

There are several reasons why it seems unlikely that Kissinger will respond to critiques of *World Order*. First, the book was published in September 2014 and so there has not been a lot of time for a critical academic engagement of the topic, largely because it can take over a year for academic book reviews to make their way through the peer review editing process.

Secondly, as a major public figure, Kissinger is not someone who tends to respond to criticism, especially from individuals such as the international relations scholar Anne-Marie Slaughter* with whom he disagrees on ideological grounds. That is not his style; rather, Kissinger is the type of scholar who publishes a book and then travels around the world giving public talks at highly regarded universities and institutions, often carefully orchestrated so that questions are searching but not overtly hostile.

A final reason why Kissinger is unlikely to respond to criticism of his text is that at his advanced age, he is unlikely to change his views even when confronted with the most persuasive alternative. As a result, it seems highly unlikely that a critical dialogue between Kissinger and his critics will ever take place over this text.

Conflict and Consensus

A more plausible intellectual outcome of the text's publication is an advance of the debate between realists and idealists, who have different conceptions of world order. Realists like Kissinger believe that foreign policy needs to reflect an assertion of power, which in turn needs to rest on legitimacy.* For example, even though Kissinger supported the US-led invasion of Iraq in 2003 that led to the Iraq War,* believing that the United States needed to project its power following the terrorist attacks of September 11, 2001 (9/11),* he also recognized that the absence of weapons of mass destruction* destroyed the legitimacy of this policing action. In short, power is not enough in itself; it must also be legitimate. To those who subscribe to Kissinger's world view, of whom there are many, the projection of power trumps any idealistic notions of cooperation.

It is at this juncture that the real debate between realists and idealists exists. For example, Anne-Marie Slaughter's outright rejection of Kissinger's work is a reflection of her belief that legitimacy takes precedence over the projection of power. In her view, foreign policy needs to be based on moral considerations and never at the expense of legitimacy. She believes that states have a responsibility to protect citizens not just at home but around the world and, if needed, states should take action to prevent atrocities, like those being committed in Syria.*6

The differences between these two camps will not be reconciled easily and will continue to shape debates about American foreign policy into the future.

NOTES

1   Daniel Marans, "Henry Kissinger Just Turned 92. Here's Why He's Careful About Where He Travels," *Huffington Post*, May 27, 2015, accessed October 9, 2015, http://www.huffingtonpost.com/2015/05/27/henry-kissinger-human-rights_n_7454172.html.

2   Hillary Clinton, "Hillary Clinton Reviews Henry Kissinger's *World Order*," *Washington Post*, September 4, 2014, accessed September 18, 2015, https://www.washingtonpost.com/opinions/hillary-clinton-reviews-henry-kissingers-world-order/2014/09/04/b280c654-31ea-11e4-8f02-03c644b2d7d0_story.html.

3   *Economist*, "A Bit of a Mess," September 6, 2014, accessed September 10, 2015, http://www.economist.com/news/books-and-arts/21615478-geopolitics-henry-kissinger-grand-and-gloomy-bit-mess.

4   Henry Kissinger, *World Order* (New York: Penguin, 2015), 325.

5   James Traub, "Book Review: World Order by Henry Kissinger," *Wall Street Journal*, September 5, 2014, accessed September 18, 2015, http://www.wsj.com/articles/book-review-world-order-by-henry-kissinger-1409952751.

6   Ann-Marie Slaughter, "How to Fix America's Foreign Policy," *New Republic*, November 19, 2014, accessed September 18, 2015, http://www.newrepublic.com/article/120030/world-order-review-what-obama-should-learn-kissingers-book.

MODULE 10
THE EVOLVING DEBATE

KEY POINTS

- It is too early to tell what *World Order* will add to the debate about how to bring about a new world order;* the book is more a history of a concept rather than the assertion of a profound argument.

- *World Order* engages directly with two main schools of thought—realism* and liberal internationalism*—while drawing on arguments from both.

- Besides its positive initial reception, *World Order* has not yet had a major impact on the debate about world order.

Uses and Problems

As one of the leading voices on American foreign policy since the early 1950s, Henry Kissinger expresses ideas in *World Order: Reflections on the Character of Nations and the Course of History* that are the product of a lifetime of scholarship, careful consideration, and debate. This analysis of an important topic—world order—from a highly respected and influential statesman, was a timely addition to an ongoing debate about how to bring about a sense of order in a world plagued with disorder.

Since the text was only published in September 2014, it is still too early to determine how Kissinger will further develop the ideas he puts forward in it. The debate over how best to forge a viable new world order has not lessened with the text's publication, with liberal internationalists arguing in favor of a strengthening of international institutions, while realists seek ways to project power, often through the use of force. More problematically, some elements in the US, such

> **❝** A values-based foreign policy can be perfectly pragmatic and prudent. It makes no sense, ever, to engage in an activity in which the costs clearly outweigh the benefits. **❞**
>
> Anne-Marie Slaughter, "How to Fix America's Foreign Policy," *New Republic*

as the neoconservatives* (those who subscribe to a political philosophy characterized by an emphasis on free-market capitalism* and an interventionist foreign policy) actively oppose liberal internationalism and have sought to undermine the very institutions that liberal internationalists are trying to build up.

While Kissinger's position on how to bring about a new world order tends to fall somewhat closer to the liberal understanding, he remains an advocate of projecting American power. It will be interesting to see if Kissinger is able to explore this position further in subsequent publications over the coming years.

Schools of Thought

Kissinger has long been a key figure in the debate among scholars of international relations, particularly among those who deal with American foreign policy, which pits realists against idealists. These two schools of thought are very broad, incorporating several subsets, and inherently antagonistic. Of the two, Kissinger is an outspoken champion of realism, but a closer examination of the ideas put forward in *World Order* suggests that he might actually represent a bridge between the two. As the former US secretary of state* Hillary Clinton* noted in her positive review of *World Order*, Kissinger believed that for an international order to take hold and last, "it must relate 'power to legitimacy.'"* To her, this admission "sounds surprisingly idealistic."[1] She is right. Though Kissinger identifies himself as a realist, he proposes that America is at its strongest when it stands up for what he believes to be American values—freedom, justice, and democracy—and its conception of world order.

To Kissinger, an important objective of US policy should be to bring about a "world order of states affirming individual dignity and participatory governance, and cooperating internationally in accordance with agreed-upon rules."[2] Even if this is a remarkably idealist objective, Kissinger is not naïve; he recognizes that the journey to a new world order will be fraught with challenges, some of which may require military force. While idealists no longer challenge this notion, the real point of contention today is under what circumstances force should be used. For modern idealists such as Anne-Marie Slaughter,* force should be used in instances where governments have failed to protect their own citizens, following the so-called Responsibility to Protect* (R2P) doctrine (the doctrine in international relations according to which a state that fails to protect its citizens from human rights violations forfeits its sovereignty,* meaning that the international community has the right to intervene). Kissinger, on the other hand, believes force should be used in instances where a nation's national interests* are threatened and efforts at diplomacy have failed to bring about a negotiated settlement.

In Current Scholarship

Although Kissinger has many admirers among America's foreign policy elite, even among those who do not typically agree with him, such as Bill Clinton,* it would be inaccurate to say that a school of thought or a group of disciples has developed around *World Order* so soon after its publication. This does not, however, mean that *World Order* does not fit in with the work of other realists, such as the international relations scholars Fareed Zakaria* or John Mearsheimer,* who both tend to approach American foreign policy questions about power, legitimacy, and national interests through the lens of history.

In June 2013, for example, Zakaria posted a video that places the Syrian civil war* in a historical context, pointing out that it is the last of three minority-dominated states in the Middle East that have undergone traumatic transitions to majority rule, following the Lebanese Civil War* (1975–90) and Iraq* after the US-led invasion in 2003, and warns that it will take at least a decade to resolve the Syrian tragedy. He uses history to argue against an American intervention in Syria, because deposing the regime would then lead to a power struggle among countless factions, of which the Islamic State of Iraq and Syria* (ISIS) is the most powerful.[3]

Mearsheimer offered a similar explanation for the crisis following the collapse of the Ukrainian* government and the subsequent annexation of the Crimean Peninsula by Russia in 2014. Arguing against the conventional wisdom that the crisis was a product of Russian aggression, Mearsheimer said that "the United States and its European allies share most of the responsibility for the crisis" due to their strategy of drawing the Ukraine* into the Western orbit, a move that Russian leaders had repeatedly opposed.[4]

NOTES

1   Hillary Clinton, "Hillary Clinton Reviews Henry Kissinger's *World Order*," *Washington Post*, September 4, 2014, accessed September 18, 2015, https://www.washingtonpost.com/opinions/hillary-clinton-reviews-henry-kissingers-world-order/2014/09/04/b280c654-31ea-11e4-8f02-03c644b2d7d0_story.html.

2   Henry Kissinger, *World Order* (New York: Penguin, 2015), 373.

3   Fareed Zakaria, "Ask Fareed Zakaria Anything: Stay Out of Syria," *The Dish*, June 7, 2013, accessed October 16, 2015, http://dish.andrewsullivan.com/2013/06/07/ask-fareed-zakaria-anything-stay-out-of-syria/.

4   John Mearsheimer, "Why the Ukraine Crisis is the West's Fault," *Foreign Affairs* (September/October 2014), accessed October 16, 2015, http://www.foreignaffairs.com/articles/141769/john-j-mearsheimer/why-the-ukraine-crisis-is-the-wests-fault.

MODULE 11
IMPACT AND INFLUENCE TODAY

KEY POINTS

- Today, *World Order* stands out as a great introductory text for students of world history and international politics.

- The main challenge to Kissinger's ideas comes from liberal internationalists* who argue that he has failed to recognize the importance of the Responsibility to Protect* doctrine (according to which the international community has the right to intervene if a state fails to protect its citizens from human rights violations).

- Kissinger has not responded directly to this challenge.

Position

As part of the contemporary debate about how to bring about a new world order,* Henry Kissinger's *World Order: Reflections on the Character of Nations and the Course of History* offers his readers a broad overview of the main issues at play, but fails to provide a thoughtful way forward. This fault seems to be by design. The text was never meant to advocate a specific set of recommendations about how the United States should force its own vision of world order on the rest of the world; rather, it looks to history to detail the challenges that future generations face in constructing such a new order. In that sense, Kissinger's text is an important guide on how to navigate modern global politics, not a remedy to the world's many problems.

For this reason, there is no set consensus as to the text's importance in terms of the wider debate between realists,* like Kissinger, and liberal internationalists, who argue that the best way to establish a new order is to strengthen international institutions.

> ❝ The irony—and enduring tragedy—of Kissinger's insistence on upholding the Westphalian norm of absolute sovereignty is that the responsibility to protect is actually an heir to the Peace of Westphalia. ❞
>
> Anne-Marie Slaughter, "How to Fix America's Foreign Policy," *New Republic*

While Kissinger is by no means opposed to international institutions like the United Nations,* his neoconservative* colleagues in the Republican Party* such as Paul Wolfowitz* or John Bolton,* do not share this view. They argue that the US needs to impose order on the world through force, as was intended to happen with the Iraq War.* In this sense, Kissinger's work emerges as a sort of bridge between the idealist* and multilateralist* vision of order on the left and the realist and unilateralist* view on the right. To Kissinger, international institutions need to be strengthened, but he also contends that states reserve the right to use force when state or non-state actors, such as the Islamic State of Iraq and Syria* (ISIS), threaten their national interests.

Interaction

As a work premised on realist assumptions, *World Order* stands somewhat opposed to liberal internationalist views of a world order premised on cooperation. The most outspoken challenger of the views expressed in Kissinger's *World Order* is Anne-Marie Slaughter,* a professor of international affairs at Princeton University who served as director of policy planning in the US department of state (the government ministry dealing with foreign affairs). She argues that Kissinger's belief in a power-based foreign policy fails to take into consideration recent progress toward the establishment of a new conception of world order in which Westphalian* principles are renovated in the form of a relatively new foreign policy concept called the Responsibility to Protect* (R2P). Slaughter believes that states have an obligation under the Universal Declaration of Human Rights* to intervene when governments are no longer able to protect their citizens. Her gripe with Kissinger stems from his "insistence on upholding the Westphalian norm of absolute sovereignty."* And that what he does not realize "is that the responsibility to protect is actually an heir to the Peace of Westphalia (1648)."*

"In an age in which the single greatest threat of the use of force against innocent civilians usually comes not from a foreign government but from their own, the responsibility to protect is an essential corollary to the Westphalian commandments. It amends the very idea of absolute sovereignty, holding states accountable at least for mass murder."[1]

In short, Slaughter argues that Kissinger fails to realize that a new world order is already beginning to take shape, largely because it does not fit with his own conception of world order.

The Continuing Debate

There is no end in sight in the ongoing debate between liberal* and neoconservative visions of world order, as the ideological divide between the two has been exacerbated by partisan politics in the United States. The centrality of the debate over world order has recently centered on the Middle East, where the rise of the Islamic State of Iraq and Syria (ISIS) has disrupted the regional order. With no end to the crisis in sight, Kissinger put forward a set of recommendations on how the Obama* administration can get itself out of a deteriorating situation in the Middle East in a recent article. He wrote: "American policy has sought to straddle the motivations of all parties and is therefore on the verge of losing the ability to shape events. The US is now opposed to, or at odds in some way or another with, all parties in the region: with Egypt on human rights; with Saudi Arabia over Yemen; with each of the Syrian parties over different objectives. The US proclaims the determination to remove [Syrian president Bashar al-Assad*] but has been unwilling to generate effective leverage—political or military—to achieve that aim."[2]

Kissinger believes that "as long as ISIS survives and remains in control of a geographically defined territory, it will compound all Middle East tensions" and argues that "the destruction of ISIS is more urgent than the overthrow of Bashar al-Assad." This proposal is firmly rooted in Kissinger's belief in the projection of American power, which is why he laments the Obama administration's acquiescence to Russia's military intervention in Syria in the fall of 2015.[3]

Slaughter takes a slightly different position. While she agrees with Kissinger that the United States needs to do something in Syria, she disagrees on the end objective. Whereas Kissinger believes the objective is destroying ISIS, Slaughter believes that it should be limited to saving the lives of innocent civilians, which is why she has called for the United States and its allies to establish a "no-fly zone" or "safe zone" in Syria to protect civilians and take steps to stave off a growing humanitarian crisis.[4]

Both of these perspectives underscore the nuanced differences between realists and liberal internationalists.

NOTES

1   Anne-Marie Slaughter, "How to Fix America's Foreign Policy," *New Republic*, November 19, 2014, accessed September 18, 2015, http://www. newrepublic.com/article/120030/world-order-review-what-obama-should-learn-kissingers-book.

2   Henry Kissinger, "A Path Out of the Middle East Collapse," *Wall Street Journal*, October 16, 2015, accessed October 22, 2015, http://www.wsj. com/articles/a-path-out-of-the-middle-east-collapse-1445037513.

3   Kissinger, "A Path Out of the Middle East Collapse."

4   Anne-Marie Slaughter, "A No-Fly Zone for Syria," *Project Syndicate*, August 25, 2015, accessed October 22, 2015, http://www.project-syndicate.org/ commentary/no-fly-zone-syria-by-anne-marie-slaughter-2015-08.

WHERE NEXT?

KEY POINTS

- *World Order* is an important and timely contribution to an ongoing debate about the nature of world order* and how to bring about a new world order.

- Looking ahead, *World Order* will continue to be an important text because it has revitalized an important debate about world order, one that had been stagnating.

- Importantly, *World Order* internationalizes the debate about the nature of world order, explaining to readers that other conceptions of world order exist that differ from their own.

Potential

Henry Kissinger's *World Order: Reflections on the Character of Nations and the Course of History* is designed for those interested in the past but concerned about the future. The text offers its readers an immensely valuable telling of world history, while explaining the origins, nuances, and challenges of some of the world's greatest civilizations. The value of this comes from the notion that the best way to predict the future is to have a strong understanding of the past. This is precisely what Kissinger's text provides for its readers.

While it seems unlikely that Kissinger will modify or update this text, it has potential to spark a debate among other diplomatic historians and scholars of international relations about how to create a new, universal world order. This is fertile ground for young scholars, who might be interested in developing theories on how to bring this about. Unfortunately, the book's conclusion fails to offer a potential strategy about what this new world order might be—which is perhaps

> ❝Kissinger's secret wish might be to stage a Congress of Vienna for the twenty-first century. And although world politics is complicated by a host of factors that don't fit easily into the Westphalian model— transnational identities, digital hyperconnectivity, weapons of mass destruction, global terrorist networks—Kissinger is still right to insist [in *World Order*] that the management of great-power relations remains of paramount importance.❞
>
> Wolfgang Ischinger, "The World According to Kissinger," *Foreign Affairs*

the spark that other scholars needed to contend with, if only by offering potential alternatives. Over time, however, it is possible that this could be an area of considerable intellectual debate.

Future Directions

At this point, it is difficult to ascertain which scholars will emerge as successors to Kissinger, particularly among those who engage in broad conceptual studies relating to concepts such as world order, sovereignty,* or balance of power.* However, it seems likely that such a successor or successors would come from the field of international relations as opposed to diplomatic history. This is because diplomatic historians, quite logically, focus on the past and rarely deal with conceptual debates about the future. While this is what separates Kissinger from most diplomatic historians, this is surely a by-product of his considerable experience as a policy-maker and his subsequent work as a political consultant for governments around the world.

In international relations, however, scholars are actively engaged in theoretical debates about the nature of relations between states, non-state actors such as international corporations and terrorist groups, and nongovernmental organizations such as the United Nations* and the World Bank.* Within this field, there are a number of theoretical variants, such as classical realism,* neorealism,* neoliberalism,* neoclassical realism,* and liberal internationalism.* Of these, neoclassical realism is the closest fit to Kissinger's outlook, realpolitik,* which focuses on maximizing power and protecting interests without concerns about morality. With this in mind, any scholar wishing to build upon Kissinger's *World Order* would probably come from this school of thought. Within the field of international relations, the most likely candidates are the political scientists John Mearsheimer,* Stephen Walt,* Robert Kagan,* Vali Nasr,* Francis Fukuyama,* and Anne-Marie Slaughter,* though in each case they would almost certainly approach the matter from different perspectives.

Summary

Kissinger's *World Order* offers an excellent insight into one of the central problems facing the world today: how to bring about a sense of order. The text presents its readers with an astute analysis of the four main views of world order: the European Westphalian* system, premised on the concepts of sovereignty, legitimacy,* and balance of power; the universalist Islamic concept of order,* which historically has pitted Muslims against non-Muslims in a competition for dominance; the Chinese system,* according to which China and its power stands as the primary source of order; and the American conception, which is rooted in the belief that freedom, justice, and democracy are universal concepts that can be applied around the world. It also offers a thought-provoking discussion of the role that technology has played as a source of inspiration (for example, in bringing people together by means of telecommunication networks) and of disruption (for example, posting videos of terrorist attacks) in the quest for world order. This discussion offers valuable insight into the challenges that world leaders face in seeking to forge a new world order.

Even though *World Order* is steeped in world history, the singular way in which Kissinger explains why each conception of world order differs from the other is valuable to anyone interested in understanding the world today—or for anyone concerned about where it is heading tomorrow.

GLOSSARY

GLOSSARY OF TERMS

9/11: on September 11, 2001, two commercial airliners hijacked by Islamic fundamentalist terrorists were flown into the World Trade Center in New York, killing approximately 3,000 people. A third hijacked airliner was crashed into the Pentagon and a fourth went down in a field in Pennsylvania.

Afghanistan War (2001–): the military intervention by North Atlantic Treaty Organization (NATO) and allied forces following the September 11 attacks on America.

Al-Qaeda: a militant Islamic fundamentalist group that was behind the terrorist attack against the United States on September 11, 2001.

American exceptionalism: a belief that the United States stands apart from other nations, largely due to an ideology based on freedom, justice, and representative democracy.

Anarchy: a state of leaderlessness; sovereign states exist in an anarchic or self-regulatory world where there is no authority compelling them one way or another.

Authoritarian: in governmental terms, a system in which governmental authority intrudes into the citizen's life at the expense of liberty.

Balance of power: in the field of international relations, the extent to which the power of one state is balanced by the equivalent power of another state or states.

Berlin Wall: a barrier that divided Berlin from 1961 to 1989 and came to symbolize the efforts of the Soviet Union to block itself and its satellite states from the West.

Boko Haram: an Islamic militant group founded in 2002 and operating in northern Nigeria. It has been fighting an insurgency since 2009, but captured global attention in April 2014 when it kidnapped 276 young girls from a school.

Capitalism: an economic system in which privately owned goods and services are exchanged for profit.

Classical realism: a school of international relations theory that assumes state action is agent-driven (controlled by leaders, rather than the structure of the system), and identifies the inherent imperfections of human nature as the source of conflict.

Cold War (1947–91): a period of tension between the United States and its Western allies and the Eastern federation of countries known as the Soviet Union, marked by the threat of nuclear war, proxy conflicts (meaning conflicts started by two nations that do not directly engage with each other), espionage, and so on.

Colonialism: refers to a policy whereby one country takes full or partial political control over another country and occupies it with colonists. It often involved unequal power relations between the ruler (colonist) and ruled (colony), and the economic exploitation of the colonies.

Communism: a political ideology that advocates state ownership of the means of production, the collectivization of labor, and the abolition of social class. It was the ideology of the Soviet Union (1922–91) and stood in contrast to free-market capitalism during the Cold War.

Confucianism: an Asian philosophical and ethical system founded by the Chinese philosopher Confucius 2,500 years ago.

Congress of Vienna (1814–15): an international conference held in Vienna, Austria, before and after the final defeat of the French emperor and military leader Napoleon Bonaparte. The conference's purpose was to reestablish a stable political order and balance of power in Europe.

Dar al-harb: the "realm of war"; a historical term denoting the territories of non-Muslims bordering *dar al-Islam* that needed to be incorporated into the Islamic empire.

Dar al-Islam: "house of Islam"; that is, the territories of the Islamic empire that emerged in the seventh century.

Détente: a policy implemented by the United States between 1969 and 1979 to deal with the Soviet Union. The policy consisted of easing tensions through less provocative behavior and interaction through meetings and summits.

Eastern Bloc: refers to a grouping of communist states, mostly in Eastern Europe, which were dominated by the Soviet Union until the late 1980s.

Ebola virus outbreak: an epidemic of the Ebola virus that swept through West Africa in 2014 killing almost 25,000 people, creating a worldwide panic that it could spread.

Geostrategy: the study of the ways in which strategy and geography shape politics and international relations.

GI Bill: a piece of US legislation adopted during World War II that provided benefits to ex-servicemen, such as low-interest loans and bursaries to cover living expenses and the costs of further education tuition.

Greenpeace: founded in Canada in 1971, it is an international organization that uses civil disobedience as a tactic to bring about awareness of environmental issues to the public and world leaders.

Hegemony: a situation where a single state or individual is able to dominate all others. For example, in the aftermath of the Cold War the United States was considered the global hegemon.

Hinduism: is a major polytheistic (that is, a belief in more than one god) world religion, practiced by over a billion people worldwide; its heartland is in the Indian subcontinent.

Holy Roman Empire: a central European political body composed of a number of states, formed during the early medieval period and dissolved in the first decade of the nineteenth century.

Idealism: a theory of international relations holding that states should apply their own internal philosophy to the conduct of international relations. This theory is closely associated with the 28th US president Woodrow Wilson, in office between 1913 and 1921, who argued that all people should have the right to determine their own destiny.

Iran's nuclear program: since the early 1990s, Western powers have accused Iran of developing nuclear weapons. The Iranian government has maintained that it has a right to develop peaceful nuclear technology and has denied a nuclear weapons programme. Negotiations about the issue have taken place periodically since 2003.

Iraq War (2003–11): an armed conflict primarily between the United States and its allies and Iraq. After toppling the government of Saddam Hussein in 2003, the conflict descended into a sectarian civil war, which pitted Iraq's Shi'a and Sunni populations against each other. In December 2011, American forces withdrew from Iraq.

Islamic State of Iraq and Syria (ISIS): a radical Islamist militant group that seized control of large swathes of territory in Iraq and Syria in 2014, and is also known to operate in eastern Libya, the Sinai Peninsula of Egypt, and other areas of the Middle East and North Africa.

Jihad: an Islamic term that means "struggle." Often mistranslated as holy war, it means to struggle against an obstacle, whether against nonbelievers or with any kind of challenge in life.

Lebanese Civil War (1975–90): a conflict waged in Lebanon after the collapse of central authority in 1975.

Legitimacy: to be lawful; to be accepted as lawful.

Liberal: as a political philosophy, liberalism emphasizes the importance of individual liberty and equality; its roots are in the period of European intellectual history known as the Enlightenment (late-seventeenth to late-eighteenth century), in which oppressive and hereditary forms of governmental power were challenged.

Liberal internationalism: a school of international relations theory that suggests states can achieve peace and mutual cooperation if policies promoting international structures fostering a liberal world order are pursued.

Limited war: a military concept used to describe a type of warfare, where strategic objectives and the scale of effort are limited. This concept is often contrasted with total war, where all the resources of a nation are geared toward ensuring total victory over an opponent. World War II is the best example of total war, whereas the 1990–91 Gulf War was limited to forcing Iraq to withdraw from Kuwait.

Malaysia Airlines Flight 370: on March 8, 2014 an airplane from the Malaysian capital, Kuala Lumpur, disappeared, leading to one of the largest search missions in history. No survivors were found, and only a small piece of wreckage was located more than a year later.

Manifest destiny: a doctrine developed in the nineteenth century in the United States that was used to justify the expansion of the country westward across North America.

Multilateralism: three or more nations working together toward an objective. Contrasted with bilateral (between two nations) or unilateral (a nation alone).

Multiplicity: a concept used to describe a situation where there are multiple poles of power in a given region (Asia, for example, where Russia, China, India, and Japan are all considered centers of power).

Multipolarity: a distribution of power within the international system; a multipolar system has power concentrated among three or more states. A bipolar system has power concentrated in two states, and a unipolar system is the dominance of a single state (also known as hegemony).

Mutually assured destruction: a phrase used during the Cold War to describe the belief that an attack by one superpower on the other would lead to the destruction of both, as each possessed the ability to launch retaliatory attacks after the first strike through nuclear armed aircraft or submarines.

National interests: a concept in international relations that describes something a state believes is vital to its political, military, economic, or diplomatic reputation or survival.

National security advisor: the chief advisor to the president of the United States for matters related to national security, foreign policy, and defense.

Nazi Germany (1933–45): Germany under the rule of Adolf Hitler, an extreme nationalist politician who sought to unify all the German-speaking people under one state and revise the European and global order. Hitler's aggressive and anti-Semitic policies led to World War II, the Holocaust (the systematic slaughter of millions of European Jews) and the deaths of perhaps 50 million people.

Neoclassical realism: a combination of neorealism and classical realism. Its supporters hold that state action can be explained with reference to both structural factors (such as the distribution of capabilities—military, economic, political, etc.—between states) and agent-driven factors (such as the ambitions of given leaders).

Neoconservatism: a political ideology characterized by an emphasis on free-market capitalism and an interventionist foreign policy. Examples of prominent neoconservatives are Paul Wolfowitz, Donald Rumsfeld, and John Bolton.

Neoliberalism: a school of international relations theory holding that cooperation among countries is possible and likely, especially through international institutions, because states prefer to maximize their absolute gains rather than their relative gains over one another.

Neorealism: a school of international relations theory assuming that structural constraints (like the distribution of world power) rather than human agency will determine actor behavior.

Nobel Peace Prize: an annual prize awarded to an individual or individuals who have devoted themselves to bringing about peaceful relations between nations. Notable winners include Henry Kissinger, Martin Luther King, Jr., Nelson Mandela, Jimmy Carter, Barack Obama, and Malala Yousafzai.

Offensive realism: a theoretical concept according to which the international system is anarchical; great powers are the main actors in global politics; all states possess offensive capabilities; another state's intentions can never be certain; survival is the primary objective; and all states are rational actors (that is, primarily concerned with their own interests).

Othering: the process of creating a collective identity ("Islamic Iran," for example) against an imaginative construction (in this case, "the Christian West"). This approach (good vs. evil, capitalism vs. communism, and so on) is often used in international relations, where states point out the negative attributes of their neighbors to emphasize their own strengths.

Peace of Westphalia (1648): a series of peace accords that ended the Thirty Years' War, signed simultaneously in Osnabrück and Münster in Germany. It helped to solidify the modern world order, whereby all states are considered equal and interstate aggression was to be solved by the establishment of a balance of power.

Realism: a school of international relations theory according to which states are the primary actors; states all share the goal of survival; and states provide for their own security.

Realpolitik: a German term meaning, literally, "the politics of real things" denoting a concept in international relations that policy decisions should be driven by pragmatic—not moral or ideological—considerations.

Republican Party: a right-wing political party in the United States founded in 1854; former Republican presidents include George H. W. Bush, George W. Bush, Richard Nixon, and Ronald Reagan.

Responsibility to Protect (RTP): a concept in international relations arguing that a state that fails to protect its citizens from human-rights violations forfeits its sovereignty and that the international community accordingly has the right to intervene.

Secretary of state: the head of the US department of state; a cabinet level position in the US government; and the chief American diplomat.

Shi'i and Sunni Islam: the two main branches of Islam, a religion that split into two main factions after the death of the Prophet Muhammad in C.E. 632. Sunni Islam is the largest religious denomination of any world religion. Shi'a Islam (sometimes written as Shia in English) or shi'ism, is the second largest sect of Islam, with a minority of around 11 percent. The differences between the sects are mostly derived from their different historical experiences, political and social developments, and ethnic composition. Shi'ites reject the first three Sunni caliphs (leaders) and regard the fourth caliph, Ali, as the prophet's true successor.

Sino-centric: an ideology holding that China stands at the center of the world.

Sovereignty: the right to govern a specific territory.

Soviet Union (1922–91): the Union of Soviet Socialist Republics (USSR), often shortened to "Soviet Union," had its roots in the Russian Revolution of 1917, which overthrew the czarist regime of the Russian Empire. In 1922, a Communist regime led by Vladimir Lenin established the Soviet Union after prevailing in a military conflict against anti-revolution parties.

Superpower: a term, first coined in 1944, to describe an exceptionally powerful and influential nation, often used to refer to the United States and the Soviet Union during the Cold War, when both states were the two most powerful nations in the world.

Syrian Civil War (2011–): a civil conflict in Syria that began as part of the Arab Spring in 2010. The conflict is between the Alawite-dominated Ba'thist Syrian government of Bashar al-Assad and several Sunni factions, which are backed by a range of foreign powers such as the United States and the Gulf States. However, beginning in 2014 the Islamic State emerged as the most powerful nongovernmental faction.

Thirty Years' War (1618-48): a European conflict between the Holy Roman Empire and several Protestant Germanic states that escalated into a near Europe-wide conflict.

Triple Éntente: an alliance formed originally between Britain, the Russian Empire, and France in 1907 in response to the growth of German power in Europe. This alliance lasted through World War I.

Ukraine War (2014–): a war that began following the collapse of the Ukrainian government when Russia annexed the Crimean Peninsula and occupied parts of eastern Ukraine.

Unification of Germany: the incorporation of all the small Germanic states of central Europe into a single German state under Wilhelm I of Prussia, head of state of the most powerful nation, Prussia. It significantly altered the balance of power in Europe.

Unilateralism: a concept in international relations used to describe a situation in which a nation acts alone.

United Nations: an international organization of countries set up in 1945 to promote international peace, security, and cooperation.

United Nations Security Council: permanent body of the United Nations looking to maintain peace and security. It consists of 15 members, of which 5 (China, France, Russia, the UK, and the US) are permanent and have the power of veto. The other members are elected for two-year terms.

Universal Declaration of Human Rights: a resolution adopted by the United Nations in 1948 that establishes a universal description of basic human rights.

Universalist Islamic order: A conception of Islam as a universalist religion, meaning that its adherents believe their view is absolute and that anyone who does not share their religion is an infidel.

Vietnam War (1955–75): a Cold War conflict between the United States and the communist forces of North Vietnam. In 1973 the US signed a peace treaty and withdrew its forces from South Vietnam, which collapsed two years later.

War on Terror: a term commonly applied to American-led actions throughout the Middle East against non-state "terrorist" actors, including al-Qaeda, following the attacks on the World Trade Center on September 11, 2001. The drone campaign in Pakistan, the occupation of Afghanistan, and other covert and overt operations are rolled into this effort.

Weapons of mass destruction: a term referring to weaponry capable of killing large amounts of people easily. It typically refers to biological, chemical, or nuclear weapons.

Weimar Republic: the constitutional state that was formed following the defeat of Germany in World War I and lasted until the coming to power of Adolf Hitler in 1933.

Westphalian system: the order governing European international relations since the signing of the peace accords of 1648 that ended the Thirty Years' War, signed simultaneously in Osnabrück and Münster in Germany. According to the accords, states are considered equal and interstate aggression was to be solved by the establishment of a balance of power. The system, imposed on the rest of the world during the colonial period, is premised on the concepts of sovereignty, legitimacy, and balance of power.

World Bank: an international financial institution originally set up in the aftermath of World War II to help finance the reconstruction of Europe. Today, it is used to help developing countries receive loans aimed at development projects and reducing poverty.

World order: roughly, a stable system governing international relations based on consensus regarding the obligations and the limits of national power and so on.

World War I (1914–18): a global conflict fought between the Central Powers (Germany, Austria–Hungary, and the Ottoman Empire) and the victorious Allied Powers (Britain, France, Russia, and, after 1917, the United States). More than 16 million people would die as a result of the war.

World War II (1939–45): a global conflict fought between the Axis powers (Germany, Italy, and Japan) and the victorious Allied powers (United Kingdom and its colonies, France, the Soviet Union, and the United States).

World Wildlife Fund: a nongovernmental organization that promotes biodiversity, conservation, and limiting the environmental impact that humans have on the planet.

PEOPLE MENTIONED IN THE TEXT

Aristotle (384–322 B.C.E.) was a Greek philosopher. Together with his teacher, Plato, he is one of the key originators of Western philosophy. Most of Aristotle's extant works, such as *Nicomachean Ethics* and *Metaphysics*, are treatises written for educational purposes in his school, the Lyceum.

Bashar al-Assad (b. 1965) has been the president of Syria since 2000. The second-born son of Hafez al-Assad, he originally trained as a doctor of ophthalmology but was named heir to his president father after his older brother died unexpectedly in 1994.

John Bolton (b. 1948) is a neoconservative political commentator and diplomat, who served as the US ambassador to the United Nations from August 2005 until December 2006.

Napoleon Bonaparte (1769–1821) was among the youngest and most successful generals of revolutionary France in the 1790s. In 1804, he declared himself emperor of the French and, following a series of shattering victories, established French domination over much of continental Europe. He was defeated at the Battle of Waterloo in 1815 and exiled to St. Helena in the South Atlantic.

Stephen Brooks is an associate professor of government at Dartmouth College. He is known for his collaboration with William Wohlforth, and his book *Producing Security: Multinational Corporations, Globalization, and the Changing Calculus of Conflict*.

George H. W. Bush (b. 1924) was the 41st president of the United States, vice-president to Ronald Reagan, served as director of the Central Intelligence Agency, and was a diplomat.

George W. Bush (b. 1946) was the 43rd president of the United States. He served two terms, from 2001 to 2009.

Jimmy Carter (b. 1924) was the 39th president of the United States. He is best known for presiding over the Iranian Revolution.

Lord Castlereagh was an Irish and British statesman, and secretary of state for foreign affairs. He is best remembered for representing Britain at the Congress of Vienna in 1814–15.

Bill Clinton (b. 1946) was the 42nd president of the United States, in office from 1993 to 2001.

Hillary Clinton (b. 1947) is an American politician and diplomat. Secretary of state between 2009 and 2013, she became a candidate in the 2016 presidential elections.

Dwight D. Eisenhower (1890–1969) was the 34th president of the United States and commanding general of the Allied forces during World War II.

William Y. Elliott (1896–1979) was a prominent American historian, who served on the US National Security Council staff following World War II, and advised six American presidents. He was Henry Kissinger's mentor at Harvard.

Gerald Ford (1913–2006) was the 38th president of the United States. He was a member of the House of Representatives until 1973, when he was selected as President Richard Nixon's vice-president after a scandal forced the resignation of his predecessor, Spiro Agnew. He became president upon Nixon's resignation in August 1974.

Francis Fukuyama (b. 1952) is an American political scientist, political economist, and author.

Adolf Hitler (1889–1945) was leader of the Nazi Party and dictator of Germany 1933–1945. His expansionist policies provoked World War II.

Samuel P. Huntington (1927–2008) was a professor of international relations at Harvard University. His book, *The Clash of Civilizations and the Remaking of World Order* is widely considered the most influential post-Cold War analysis of international order.

Wolfgang Ischinger (b. 1946) is a German diplomat, who served as the German ambassador to the United States from 2001 to 2006.

Robert Kagan (b. 1958) is an American neoconservative political commentator, who has served as an advisor to Hillary Clinton, John Kerry, and John McCain.

Immanuel Kant (1724–1804) was a Prussian philosopher (what is now modern Germany), who was best known for his defense of the idea that all people were worthy of equal consideration and respect, based on the idea that one should act as though one's actions were the universal law (the "categorical imperative").

Paul Kennedy (b. 1945) is a British-born professor of history at Yale University, who is known for his work on international relations. He is best known for his book *The Rise and Fall of the Great Powers* (1987).

Robert Keohane (b. 1941) is an American political science professor at Princeton. He is associated with neoliberal institutionalism—based on the notion that international institutions can encourage cooperation between states—and, notably, wrote *Power and Interdependence* with Joseph Nye.

Fritz Kraemer (1908–2003) was a German-born American military advisor, who convinced close friend Henry Kissinger to further his education.

Niccolò Machiavelli (1469–1527) was an Italian philosopher and diplomat, best known as the author of *The Prince*, in which he argued that the use of force and immoral behavior are sometimes necessary to retain power; this is justifiable because no means should be spared to achieve this end.

John Mearsheimer (b. 1947) is a professor of international relations at the University of Chicago. His 2001 work, *The Tragedy of Great Power Politics*, established him as a leading international relations theorist in the neorealist school of political thought. This text introduced the theory of offensive realism.

Klemens Wenzel von Metternich (1773–1859) was an Austrian prince, diplomat, and state chancellor between 1821 and 1848. He played a pivotal role in bringing about the Congress of Vienna, which established a new order in Europe.

Hans Morgenthau (1904–80) was a German political theorist who worked primarily in America. He has been described as the most prominent of the classical realists.

Prophet Muhammad (c.e. 570–632) was the founder of Islam. Starting in 610, he experience a series of prophetic experiences that were later transcribed into the Islamic holy book, the Koran, which became the basis of Islamic doctrine and legislation (*shari'a*).

Vali Nasr (b. 1960) is an American political scientist who specializes in the international relations of the Middle East. He is currently the dean of the School of Advanced International Studies at Johns Hopkins University.

Richard Nixon (1913–94) was the 37th president of the United States and the first American president to resign from office, having been embroiled in the Watergate scandal.

Joseph Nye, Jr. (b. 1937) is an American political science professor at Harvard. Together with Robert Keohane he wrote *Power and Interdependence* (1977), effectively founding neoliberal institutionalism.

Barack Obama (b. 1961) is the 44th president of the United States and was elected in 2008. He is the country's first black president.

Lord Palmerston (1784–1865) was prime minister of Britain from 1855 to 1858 and from 1859 to 1865.

Leopold von Ranke (1795–1886) was a German historian who founded a methodological approach aimed at developing historical narratives based on archival research.

Nelson Rockefeller (1908–79) was the 41st vice-president of the United States, the 49th governor of New York, a prominent American businessman, and a philanthropist; he hailed from the wealthy Rockefeller family.

Theodore Roosevelt (1858–1919) was the 26th president of the United States. He is best known for his association with the realist school of thought.

Anne-Marie Slaughter (b. 1958) is a professor of politics and international affairs at Princeton, a foreign-policy analyst, and currently the president of the New America Foundation.

Benedict de Spinoza (1632–77) was a Jewish Dutch philosopher in the rationalist tradition. His main works are *Tractatus Logico-Politicus* and *Ethics*.

Joseph Stalin (1878–1953) led the Soviet Union from 1924 to 1953 and was responsible for the deaths of millions through political purges and coercive economic policies.

Thucydides (c. 460–395 B.C.E.) was a Greek historian, best known for a chronicle of the 431–404 B.C.E. war between Athens and Sparta entitled *The History of the Peloponnesian War.* He is considered to be one of the first proponents of "realpolitik," the idea that power and interests should take precedence over ideas and ethics in politics.

James Traub (b. 1954) is an American journalist who specializes in international affairs and writes for the *New York Times.*

Stephen Walt (b. 1955) is a professor of international relations at Harvard University and a leading international relations theorist from the neorealist school of political thought. He developed the theoretical concept known as "balance of threat."

Woodrow Wilson (1856–1924) was the 28th president of the United States of America, from 1913 to 1921. He is best known for his liberal idealist principles and his role in attempting to reconstruct Europe on democratic principles after World War I.

William Wohlforth (b. 1959) is an American professor of government at Dartmouth College. He is best known for his collaborations with Stephen Brooks, and his text *The Elusive Balance: Power and Perceptions during the Cold War* (1993).

Paul Wolfowitz (b. 1943) is a neoconservative scholar, a former president of the World Bank, and was a deputy secretary of defense during the George W. Bush administration. He played a pivotal role in bringing about the ill-fated Iraq War.

Fareed Zakaria (b. 1964) is an Indian American journalist, author, and neorealist scholar. He has been managing editor of *Foreign Affairs*, editor-at- large at *Time* and, notably, authored *The Post-American World*.

WORKS CITED

Arms Control Association. "Iran Nuclear Negotiations: Separating Myth from Reality." *Issue Briefs* 7, no. 2 (January 2015). Accessed November 4, 2015. https://www.armscontrol.org/issue-briefs/2015-01-23/Iran-Nuclear-Negotiations-Separating-Myth-from-Reality.

Brooks, Stephen G., and William C. Wohlforth. "Reshaping the World Order." *Foreign Affairs* (March/April 2009): 49–63. Accessed December 7, 2015. https://www.foreignaffairs.com/articles/2009-03-01/reshaping-world-order.

Centers for Disease Control and Prevention. "2014 Ebola Outbreak in West Africa – Case Counts." Accessed November 18, 2015. http://www.cdc.gov/vhf/ebola/outbreaks/2014-west-africa/case-counts.html.

Clinton, Hillary R. "Hillary Clinton Reviews Henry Kissinger's *World Order*." *Washington Post*, September 4, 2014. Accessed September 18, 2015. https://www.washingtonpost.com/opinions/hillary-clinton-reviews-henry-kissingers-world-order/2014/09/04/b280c654-31ea-11e4-8f02-03c644b2d7d0_story.html.

Dallek, Robert. *Nixon and Kissinger: Partners in Power*. London: HarperCollins, 2007.

Drezner, Daniel W. "The New New World Order." *Foreign Affairs* (March/April 2007): 34–46. Accessed December 7, 2015. https://www.foreignaffairs.com/articles/2007-03-01/new-new-world-order.

Economist. "A Bit of a Mess," September 6, 2014. Accessed September 10, 2015. http://www.economist.com/news/books-and-arts/21615478-geopolitics-henry-kissinger-grand-and-gloomy-bit-mess.

Fukuyama, Francis. *The End of History and the Last Man*. New York: Free Press, 2006.

Hitchens, Christopher. *The Trial of Henry Kissinger*. London: Verso, 2001.

Huntington, Samuel. "The Clash of Civilizations?" *Foreign Affairs* (Summer 1993): 22–49. Accessed December 7, 2015. https://www.foreignaffairs.com/articles/united-states/1993-06-01/clash-civilizations.

The Clash of Civilizations and the Remaking of World Order. New York: Simon and Schuster, 1996.

Ischinger, Wolfgang. "The World According to Kissinger: How to Defend Global Order." *Foreign Affairs* (March/April 2015). Accessed October 1, 2015. https://www.foreignaffairs.com/reviews/2015-03-01/world-according-kissinger.

Kennedy, Paul. *The Parliament of Man: The Past, Present, and Future of the United Nations.* New York: Random House, 2006.

Kissinger, Henry. "A Path Out of the Middle East Collapse." *Wall Street Journal*, October 16, 2015. Accessed October 22, 2015. http://www.wsj.com/articles/a-path-out-of-the-middle-east-collapse-1445037513.

A World Restored: Metternich, Castlereagh and the Problems of Peace, 1812–22. New York: Weidenfeld and Nicolson, 1957.

American Foreign Policy: Three Essays. New York: W. W. Norton, 1969.

Diplomacy. New York: Simon and Schuster, 1994.

Nuclear Weapons and Foreign Policy. New York: Harper & Brothers, 1957.

On China. New York: Penguin, 2011.

The Necessity for Choice: Prospects of American Foreign Policy. New York: Doubleday, 1961.

The Troubled Partnership: A Reappraisal of the Atlantic Alliance. New York: McGraw-Hill, 1965.

White House Years. Boston: Little, Brown, 1979.

World Order. New York: Penguin, 2015.

Years of Renewal. New York: Simon and Schuster, 1999.

Years of Upheaval. Boston: Little, Brown, 1982.

Marans, Daniel. "Henry Kissinger Just Turned 92. Here's Why He's Careful About Where He Travels." *Huffington Post*, May 27, 2015. Accessed October 9, 2015. http://www.huffingtonpost.com/2015/05/27/henry-kissinger-human-rights_n_7454172.html.

Mearsheimer, John J. *The Tragedy of Great Power Politics*. New York: W. W. Norton, 2001.

"Why The Ukraine Crisis is the West's Fault." *Foreign Affairs* (September/October 2014). Accessed October 16, 2015. http://www.foreignaffairs.com/articles/141769/john-j-mearsheimer/why-the-ukraine-crisis-is-the-wests-fault.

Micklethwait, John. "As the World Turns: Henry Kissinger's 'World Order.'" *New York Times*, September 11, 2014. Accessed December 7, 2015. http://www.nytimes.com/2014/09/14/books/review/henry-kissingers-world-order.html?_r=0.

Mitter, Rana. "'World Order' by Henry Kissinger – review." *Guardian*, October 1, 2014. Accessed October 15, 2015. http://www.theguardian.com/books/2014/oct/01/world-order-by-henry-kissinger-review-account.

Morgenthau, Hans. *Politics Among Nations: The Struggle for Power and Peace.* New York: Knopf, 1948.

"Review: *Nuclear Weapons and Foreign Policy* by Henry Kissinger." *American Political Science Review* 52, no. 3 (September 1958): 842–4.

Nye, Jr., Joseph S. "What New World Order?" *Foreign Affairs* (Spring 1992): 83–96. Accessed December 7, 2015. https://www.foreignaffairs.com/articles/1992-03-01/what-new-world-order.

Slaughter, Anne-Marie. "A No-Fly Zone for Syria." *Project Syndicate*, August 25, 2015. Accessed October 22, 2015. http://www.project-syndicate.org/commentary/no-fly-zone-syria-by-anne-marie-slaughter-2015-08.

"How to Fix America's Foreign Policy." *New Republic*, November 19, 2014. Accessed September 18, 2015. http://www.newrepublic.com/article/120030/world-order-review-what-obama-should-learn-kissingers-book.

"The Real New World Order." *Foreign Affairs* (September/October 1997): 183–97. Accessed December 7, 2015. https://www.foreignaffairs.com/articles/1997-09-01/real-new-world-order.

Traub, James. "Book Review: *World Order* by Henry Kissinger." *Wall Street Journal*, September 5, 2014. Accessed September 18, 2015. http://www.wsj.com/articles/book-review-world-order-by-henry-kissinger-1409952751.

Zakaria, Fareed. "Ask Fareed Zakaria Anything: Stay Out of Syria." *The Dish*, June 7, 2013. Accessed October 16, 2015. http://dish.andrewsullivan.com/2013/06/07/ask-fareed-zakaria-anything-stay-out-of-syria/.

THE MACAT LIBRARY
BY DISCIPLINE

The Macat Library By Discipline

AFRICANA STUDIES

Chinua Achebe's *An Image of Africa: Racism in Conrad's Heart of Darkness*
W. E. B. Du Bois's *The Souls of Black Folk*
Zora Neale Huston's *Characteristics of Negro Expression*
Martin Luther King Jr's *Why We Can't Wait*
Toni Morrison's *Playing in the Dark: Whiteness in the American Literary Imagination*

ANTHROPOLOGY

Arjun Appadurai's *Modernity at Large: Cultural Dimensions of Globalisation*
Philippe Ariès's *Centuries of Childhood*
Franz Boas's *Race, Language and Culture*
Kim Chan & Renée Mauborgne's *Blue Ocean Strategy*
Jared Diamond's *Guns, Germs & Steel: the Fate of Human Societies*
Jared Diamond's *Collapse: How Societies Choose to Fail or Survive*
E. E. Evans-Pritchard's *Witchcraft, Oracles and Magic Among the Azande*
James Ferguson's *The Anti-Politics Machine*
Clifford Geertz's *The Interpretation of Cultures*
David Graeber's *Debt: the First 5000 Years*
Karen Ho's *Liquidated: An Ethnography of Wall Street*
Geert Hofstede's *Culture's Consequences: Comparing Values, Behaviors, Institutes and Organizations across Nations*
Claude Lévi-Strauss's *Structural Anthropology*
Jay Macleod's *Ain't No Makin' It: Aspirations and Attainment in a Low-Income Neighborhood*
Saba Mahmood's *The Politics of Piety: The Islamic Revival and the Feminist Subject*
Marcel Mauss's *The Gift*

BUSINESS

Jean Lave & Etienne Wenger's *Situated Learning*
Theodore Levitt's *Marketing Myopia*
Burton G. Malkiel's *A Random Walk Down Wall Street*
Douglas McGregor's *The Human Side of Enterprise*
Michael Porter's *Competitive Strategy: Creating and Sustaining Superior Performance*
John Kotter's *Leading Change*
C. K. Prahalad & Gary Hamel's *The Core Competence of the Corporation*

CRIMINOLOGY

Michelle Alexander's *The New Jim Crow: Mass Incarceration in the Age of Colorblindness*
Michael R. Gottfredson & Travis Hirschi's *A General Theory of Crime*
Richard Herrnstein & Charles A. Murray's *The Bell Curve: Intelligence and Class Structure in American Life*
Elizabeth Loftus's *Eyewitness Testimony*
Jay Macleod's *Ain't No Makin' It: Aspirations and Attainment in a Low-Income Neighborhood*
Philip Zimbardo's *The Lucifer Effect*

ECONOMICS

Janet Abu-Lughod's *Before European Hegemony*
Ha-Joon Chang's *Kicking Away the Ladder*
David Brion Davis's *The Problem of Slavery in the Age of Revolution*
Milton Friedman's *The Role of Monetary Policy*
Milton Friedman's *Capitalism and Freedom*
David Graeber's *Debt: the First 5000 Years*
Friedrich Hayek's *The Road to Serfdom*
Karen Ho's *Liquidated: An Ethnography of Wall Street*

John Maynard Keynes's *The General Theory of Employment, Interest and Money*
Charles P. Kindleberger's *Manias, Panics and Crashes*
Robert Lucas's *Why Doesn't Capital Flow from Rich to Poor Countries?*
Burton G. Malkiel's *A Random Walk Down Wall Street*
Thomas Robert Malthus's *An Essay on the Principle of Population*
Karl Marx's *Capital*
Thomas Piketty's *Capital in the Twenty-First Century*
Amartya Sen's *Development as Freedom*
Adam Smith's *The Wealth of Nations*
Nassim Nicholas Taleb's *The Black Swan: The Impact of the Highly Improbable*
Amos Tversky's & Daniel Kahneman's *Judgment under Uncertainty: Heuristics and Biases*
Mahbub Ul Haq's *Reflections on Human Development*
Max Weber's *The Protestant Ethic and the Spirit of Capitalism*

FEMINISM AND GENDER STUDIES

Judith Butler's *Gender Trouble*
Simone De Beauvoir's *The Second Sex*
Michel Foucault's *History of Sexuality*
Betty Friedan's *The Feminine Mystique*
Saba Mahmood's *The Politics of Piety: The Islamic Revival and the Feminist Subjec*t
Joan Wallach Scott's *Gender and the Politics of History*
Mary Wollstonecraft's *A Vindication of the Rights of Woman*
Virginia Woolf's *A Room of One's Own*

GEOGRAPHY

The Brundtland Report's *Our Common Future*
Rachel Carson's *Silent Spring*
Charles Darwin's *On the Origin of Species*
James Ferguson's *The Anti-Politics Machine*
Jane Jacobs's *The Death and Life of Great American Cities*
James Lovelock's *Gaia: A New Look at Life on Earth*
Amartya Sen's *Development as Freedom*
Mathis Wackernagel & William Rees's *Our Ecological Footprint*

HISTORY

Janet Abu-Lughod's *Before European Hegemony*
Benedict Anderson's *Imagined Communities*
Bernard Bailyn's *The Ideological Origins of the American Revolution*
Hanna Batatu's *The Old Social Classes And The Revolutionary Movements Of Iraq*
Christopher Browning's *Ordinary Men: Reserve Police Batallion 101 and the Final Solution in Poland*
Edmund Burke's *Reflections on the Revolution in France*
William Cronon's *Nature's Metropolis: Chicago And The Great West*
Alfred W. Crosby's *The Columbian Exchange*
Hamid Dabashi's *Iran: A People Interrupted*
David Brion Davis's *The Problem of Slavery in the Age of Revolution*
Nathalie Zemon Davis's *The Return of Martin Guerre*
Jared Diamond's *Guns, Germs & Steel: the Fate of Human Societies*
Frank Dikotter's *Mao's Great Famine*
John W Dower's *War Without Mercy: Race And Power In The Pacific War*
W. E. B. Du Bois's *The Souls of Black Folk*
Richard J. Evans's *In Defence of History*
Lucien Febvre's *The Problem of Unbelief in the 16th Century*
Sheila Fitzpatrick's *Everyday Stalinism*

The Macat Library By Discipline

Eric Foner's *Reconstruction: America's Unfinished Revolution, 1863-1877*
Michel Foucault's *Discipline and Punish*
Michel Foucault's *History of Sexuality*
Francis Fukuyama's *The End of History and the Last Man*
John Lewis Gaddis's *We Now Know: Rethinking Cold War History*
Ernest Gellner's *Nations and Nationalism*
Eugene Genovese's *Roll, Jordan, Roll: The World the Slaves Made*
Carlo Ginzburg's *The Night Battles*
Daniel Goldhagen's *Hitler's Willing Executioners*
Jack Goldstone's *Revolution and Rebellion in the Early Modern World*
Antonio Gramsci's *The Prison Notebooks*
Alexander Hamilton, John Jay & James Madison's *The Federalist Papers*
Christopher Hill's *The World Turned Upside Down*
Carole Hillenbrand's *The Crusades: Islamic Perspectives*
Thomas Hobbes's *Leviathan*
Eric Hobsbawm's *The Age Of Revolution*
John A. Hobson's *Imperialism: A Study*
Albert Hourani's *History of the Arab Peoples*
Samuel P. Huntington's *The Clash of Civilizations and the Remaking of World Order*
C. L. R. James's *The Black Jacobins*
Tony Judt's *Postwar: A History of Europe Since 1945*
Ernst Kantorowicz's *The King's Two Bodies: A Study in Medieval Political Theology*
Paul Kennedy's *The Rise and Fall of the Great Powers*
Ian Kershaw's *The "Hitler Myth": Image and Reality in the Third Reich*
John Maynard Keynes's *The General Theory of Employment, Interest and Money*
Charles P. Kindleberger's *Manias, Panics and Crashes*
Martin Luther King Jr's *Why We Can't Wait*
Henry Kissinger's *World Order: Reflections on the Character of Nations and the Course of History*
Thomas Kuhn's *The Structure of Scientific Revolutions*
Georges Lefebvre's *The Coming of the French Revolution*
John Locke's *Two Treatises of Government*
Niccolò Machiavelli's *The Prince*
Thomas Robert Malthus's *An Essay on the Principle of Population*
Mahmood Mamdani's *Citizen and Subject: Contemporary Africa And The Legacy Of Late Colonialism*
Karl Marx's *Capital*
Stanley Milgram's *Obedience to Authority*
John Stuart Mill's *On Liberty*
Thomas Paine's *Common Sense*
Thomas Paine's *Rights of Man*
Geoffrey Parker's *Global Crisis: War, Climate Change and Catastrophe in the Seventeenth Century*
Jonathan Riley-Smith's *The First Crusade and the Idea of Crusading*
Jean-Jacques Rousseau's *The Social Contract*
Joan Wallach Scott's *Gender and the Politics of History*
Theda Skocpol's *States and Social Revolutions*
Adam Smith's *The Wealth of Nations*
Timothy Snyder's *Bloodlands: Europe Between Hitler and Stalin*
Sun Tzu's *The Art of War*
Keith Thomas's *Religion and the Decline of Magic*
Thucydides's *The History of the Peloponnesian War*
Frederick Jackson Turner's *The Significance of the Frontier in American History*
Odd Arne Westad's *The Global Cold War: Third World Interventions And The Making Of Our Times*

LITERATURE

Chinua Achebe's *An Image of Africa: Racism in Conrad's Heart of Darkness*
Roland Barthes's *Mythologies*
Homi K. Bhabha's *The Location of Culture*
Judith Butler's *Gender Trouble*
Simone De Beauvoir's *The Second Sex*
Ferdinand De Saussure's *Course in General Linguistics*
T. S. Eliot's *The Sacred Wood: Essays on Poetry and Criticism*
Zora Neale Huston's *Characteristics of Negro Expression*
Toni Morrison's *Playing in the Dark: Whiteness in the American Literary Imagination*
Edward Said's *Orientalism*
Gayatri Chakravorty Spivak's *Can the Subaltern Speak?*
Mary Wollstonecraft's *A Vindication of the Rights of Women*
Virginia Woolf's *A Room of One's Own*

PHILOSOPHY

Elizabeth Anscombe's *Modern Moral Philosophy*
Hannah Arendt's *The Human Condition*
Aristotle's *Metaphysics*
Aristotle's *Nicomachean Ethics*
Edmund Gettier's *Is Justified True Belief Knowledge?*
Georg Wilhelm Friedrich Hegel's *Phenomenology of Spirit*
David Hume's *Dialogues Concerning Natural Religion*
David Hume's *The Enquiry for Human Understanding*
Immanuel Kant's *Religion within the Boundaries of Mere Reason*
Immanuel Kant's *Critique of Pure Reason*
Søren Kierkegaard's *The Sickness Unto Death*
Søren Kierkegaard's *Fear and Trembling*
C. S. Lewis's *The Abolition of Man*
Alasdair MacIntyre's *After Virtue*
Marcus Aurelius's *Meditations*
Friedrich Nietzsche's *On the Genealogy of Morality*
Friedrich Nietzsche's *Beyond Good and Evil*
Plato's *Republic*
Plato's *Symposium*
Jean-Jacques Rousseau's *The Social Contract*
Gilbert Ryle's *The Concept of Mind*
Baruch Spinoza's *Ethics*
Sun Tzu's *The Art of War*
Ludwig Wittgenstein's *Philosophical Investigations*

POLITICS

Benedict Anderson's *Imagined Communities*
Aristotle's *Politics*
Bernard Bailyn's *The Ideological Origins of the American Revolution*
Edmund Burke's *Reflections on the Revolution in France*
John C. Calhoun's *A Disquisition on Government*
Ha-Joon Chang's *Kicking Away the Ladder*
Hamid Dabashi's *Iran: A People Interrupted*
Hamid Dabashi's *Theology of Discontent: The Ideological Foundation of the Islamic Revolution in Iran*
Robert Dahl's *Democracy and its Critics*
Robert Dahl's *Who Governs?*
David Brion Davis's *The Problem of Slavery in the Age of Revolution*

The Macat Library By Discipline

Alexis De Tocqueville's *Democracy in America*
James Ferguson's *The Anti-Politics Machine*
Frank Dikotter's *Mao's Great Famine*
Sheila Fitzpatrick's *Everyday Stalinism*
Eric Foner's *Reconstruction: America's Unfinished Revolution, 1863-1877*
Milton Friedman's *Capitalism and Freedom*
Francis Fukuyama's *The End of History and the Last Man*
John Lewis Gaddis's *We Now Know: Rethinking Cold War History*
Ernest Gellner's *Nations and Nationalism*
David Graeber's *Debt: the First 5000 Years*
Antonio Gramsci's *The Prison Notebooks*
Alexander Hamilton, John Jay & James Madison's *The Federalist Papers*
Friedrich Hayek's *The Road to Serfdom*
Christopher Hill's *The World Turned Upside Down*
Thomas Hobbes's *Leviathan*
John A. Hobson's *Imperialism: A Study*
Samuel P. Huntington's *The Clash of Civilizations and the Remaking of World Order*
Tony Judt's *Postwar: A History of Europe Since 1945*
David C. Kang's *China Rising: Peace, Power and Order in East Asia*
Paul Kennedy's *The Rise and Fall of Great Powers*
Robert Keohane's *After Hegemony*
Martin Luther King Jr.'s *Why We Can't Wait*
Henry Kissinger's *World Order: Reflections on the Character of Nations and the Course of History*
John Locke's *Two Treatises of Government*
Niccolò Machiavelli's *The Prince*
Thomas Robert Malthus's *An Essay on the Principle of Population*
Mahmood Mamdani's *Citizen and Subject: Contemporary Africa And The Legacy Of Late Colonialism*
Karl Marx's *Capital*
John Stuart Mill's *On Liberty*
John Stuart Mill's *Utilitarianism*
Hans Morgenthau's *Politics Among Nations*
Thomas Paine's *Common Sense*
Thomas Paine's *Rights of Man*
Thomas Piketty's *Capital in the Twenty-First Century*
Robert D. Putman's *Bowling Alone*
John Rawls's *Theory of Justice*
Jean-Jacques Rousseau's *The Social Contract*
Theda Skocpol's *States and Social Revolutions*
Adam Smith's *The Wealth of Nations*
Sun Tzu's *The Art of War*
Henry David Thoreau's *Civil Disobedience*
Thucydides's *The History of the Peloponnesian War*
Kenneth Waltz's *Theory of International Politics*
Max Weber's *Politics as a Vocation*
Odd Arne Westad's *The Global Cold War: Third World Interventions And The Making Of Our Times*

POSTCOLONIAL STUDIES

Roland Barthes's *Mythologies*
Frantz Fanon's *Black Skin, White Masks*
Homi K. Bhabha's *The Location of Culture*
Gustavo Gutiérrez's *A Theology of Liberation*
Edward Said's *Orientalism*
Gayatri Chakravorty Spivak's *Can the Subaltern Speak?*

PSYCHOLOGY

Gordon Allport's *The Nature of Prejudice*
Alan Baddeley & Graham Hitch's *Aggression: A Social Learning Analysis*
Albert Bandura's *Aggression: A Social Learning Analysis*
Leon Festinger's *A Theory of Cognitive Dissonance*
Sigmund Freud's *The Interpretation of Dreams*
Betty Friedan's *The Feminine Mystique*
Michael R. Gottfredson & Travis Hirschi's *A General Theory of Crime*
Eric Hoffer's *The True Believer: Thoughts on the Nature of Mass Movements*
William James's *Principles of Psychology*
Elizabeth Loftus's *Eyewitness Testimony*
A. H. Maslow's *A Theory of Human Motivation*
Stanley Milgram's *Obedience to Authority*
Steven Pinker's *The Better Angels of Our Nature*
Oliver Sacks's *The Man Who Mistook His Wife For a Hat*
Richard Thaler & Cass Sunstein's *Nudge: Improving Decisions About Health, Wealth and Happiness*
Amos Tversky's *Judgment under Uncertainty: Heuristics and Biases*
Philip Zimbardo's *The Lucifer Effect*

SCIENCE

Rachel Carson's *Silent Spring*
William Cronon's *Nature's Metropolis: Chicago And The Great West*
Alfred W. Crosby's *The Columbian Exchange*
Charles Darwin's *On the Origin of Species*
Richard Dawkin's *The Selfish Gene*
Thomas Kuhn's *The Structure of Scientific Revolutions*
Geoffrey Parker's *Global Crisis: War, Climate Change and Catastrophe in the Seventeenth Century*
Mathis Wackernagel & William Rees's *Our Ecological Footprint*

SOCIOLOGY

Michelle Alexander's *The New Jim Crow: Mass Incarceration in the Age of Colorblindness*
Gordon Allport's *The Nature of Prejudice*
Albert Bandura's *Aggression: A Social Learning Analysis*
Hanna Batatu's *The Old Social Classes And The Revolutionary Movements Of Iraq*
Ha-Joon Chang's *Kicking Away the Ladder*
W. E. B. Du Bois's *The Souls of Black Folk*
Émile Durkheim's *On Suicide*
Frantz Fanon's *Black Skin, White Masks*
Frantz Fanon's *The Wretched of the Earth*
Eric Foner's *Reconstruction: America's Unfinished Revolution, 1863-1877*
Eugene Genovese's *Roll, Jordan, Roll: The World the Slaves Made*
Jack Goldstone's *Revolution and Rebellion in the Early Modern World*
Antonio Gramsci's *The Prison Notebooks*
Richard Herrnstein & Charles A Murray's *The Bell Curve: Intelligence and Class Structure in American Life*
Eric Hoffer's *The True Believer: Thoughts on the Nature of Mass Movements*
Jane Jacobs's *The Death and Life of Great American Cities*
Robert Lucas's *Why Doesn't Capital Flow from Rich to Poor Countries?*
Jay Macleod's *Ain't No Makin' It: Aspirations and Attainment in a Low Income Neighborhood*
Elaine May's *Homeward Bound: American Families in the Cold War Era*
Douglas McGregor's *The Human Side of Enterprise*
C. Wright Mills's *The Sociological Imagination*

The Macat Library By Discipline

Thomas Piketty's *Capital in the Twenty-First Century*
Robert D. Putman's *Bowling Alone*
David Riesman's *The Lonely Crowd: A Study of the Changing American Character*
Edward Said's *Orientalism*
Joan Wallach Scott's *Gender and the Politics of History*
Theda Skocpol's *States and Social Revolutions*
Max Weber's *The Protestant Ethic and the Spirit of Capitalism*

THEOLOGY

Augustine's *Confessions*
Benedict's *Rule of St Benedict*
Gustavo Gutiérrez's *A Theology of Liberation*
Carole Hillenbrand's *The Crusades: Islamic Perspectives*
David Hume's *Dialogues Concerning Natural Religion*
Immanuel Kant's *Religion within the Boundaries of Mere Reason*
Ernst Kantorowicz's *The King's Two Bodies: A Study in Medieval Political Theology*
Søren Kierkegaard's *The Sickness Unto Death*
C. S. Lewis's *The Abolition of Man*
Saba Mahmood's *The Politics of Piety: The Islamic Revival and the Feminist Subjec*t
Baruch Spinoza's *Ethics*
Keith Thomas's *Religion and the Decline of Magic*

COMING SOON

Chris Argyris's *The Individual and the Organisation*
Seyla Benhabib's *The Rights of Others*
Walter Benjamin's *The Work Of Art in the Age of Mechanical Reproduction*
John Berger's *Ways of Seeing*
Pierre Bourdieu's *Outline of a Theory of Practice*
Mary Douglas's *Purity and Danger*
Roland Dworkin's *Taking Rights Seriously*
James G. March's *Exploration and Exploitation in Organisational Learning*
Ikujiro Nonaka's *A Dynamic Theory of Organizational Knowledge Creation*
Griselda Pollock's *Vision and Difference*
Amartya Sen's *Inequality Re-Examined*
Susan Sontag's *On Photography*
Yasser Tabbaa's *The Transformation of Islamic Art*
Ludwig von Mises's *Theory of Money and Credit*

Macat Disciplines

Access the greatest ideas and thinkers across entire disciplines, including

GLOBALIZATION

Arjun Appadurai's, *Modernity at Large: Cultural Dimensions of Globalisation*

James Ferguson's, *The Anti-Politics Machine*

Geert Hofstede's, *Culture's Consequences*

Amartya Sen's, *Development as Freedom*

Macat Disciplines

Access the greatest ideas and thinkers across entire disciplines, including

THE FUTURE OF DEMOCRACY

Robert A. Dahl's, *Democracy and Its Critics*
Robert A. Dahl's, *Who Governs?*
Alexis De Toqueville's, *Democracy in America*
Niccolò Machiavelli's, *The Prince*
John Stuart Mill's, *On Liberty*
Robert D. Putnam's, *Bowling Alone*
Jean-Jacques Rousseau's, *The Social Contract*
Henry David Thoreau's, *Civil Disobedience*

Macat Disciplines

Access the greatest ideas and thinkers across entire disciplines, including

TOTALITARIANISM

Sheila Fitzpatrick's, *Everyday Stalinism*
Ian Kershaw's, *The "Hitler Myth"*
Timothy Snyder's, *Bloodlands*

Macat Pairs

Analyse historical and modern issues from opposite sides of an argument. Pairs include:

RACE AND IDENTITY

Zora Neale Hurston's
Characteristics of Negro Expression

Using material collected on anthropological expeditions to the South, Zora Neale Hurston explains how expression in African American culture in the early twentieth century departs from the art of white America. At the time, African American art was often criticized for copying white culture. For Hurston, this criticism misunderstood how art works. European tradition views art as something fixed. But Hurston describes a creative process that is alive, ever-changing, and largely improvisational. She maintains that African American art works through a process called 'mimicry'—where an imitated object or verbal pattern, for example, is reshaped and altered until it becomes something new, novel—and worthy of attention.

Frantz Fanon's
Black Skin, White Masks

Black Skin, White Masks offers a radical analysis of the psychological effects of colonization on the colonized.

Fanon witnessed the effects of colonization first hand both in his birthplace, Martinique, and again later in life when he worked as a psychiatrist in another French colony, Algeria. His text is uncompromising in form and argument. He dissects the dehumanizing effects of colonialism, arguing that it destroys the native sense of identity, forcing people to adapt to an alien set of values—including a core belief that they are inferior. This results in deep psychological trauma.

Fanon's work played a pivotal role in the civil rights movements of the 1960s.

Macat analyses are available from all good bookshops and libraries.

Access hundreds of analyses through one, multimedia tool.
Join free for one month **library.macat.com**

Macat Pairs

Analyse historical and modern issues from opposite sides of an argument. Pairs include:

INTERNATIONAL RELATIONS IN THE 21ST CENTURY

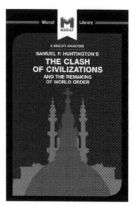

Samuel P. Huntington's
The Clash of Civilisations

In his highly influential 1996 book, Huntington offers a vision of a post-Cold War world in which conflict takes place not between competing ideologies but between cultures. The worst clash, he argues, will be between the Islamic world and the West: the West's arrogance and belief that its culture is a "gift" to the world will come into conflict with Islam's obstinacy and concern that its culture is under attack from a morally decadent "other."

Clash inspired much debate between different political schools of thought. But its greatest impact came in helping define American foreign policy in the wake of the 2001 terrorist attacks in New York and Washington.

Francis Fukuyama's
The End of History and the Last Man

Published in 1992, *The End of History and the Last Man* argues that capitalist democracy is the final destination for all societies. Fukuyama believed democracy triumphed during the Cold War because it lacks the "fundamental contradictions" inherent in communism and satisfies our yearning for freedom and equality. Democracy therefore marks the endpoint in the evolution of ideology, and so the "end of history." There will still be "events," but no fundamental change in ideology.

Macat analyses are available from all good bookshops and libraries.

Access hundreds of analyses through one, multimedia tool.

Join free for one month **library.macat.com**

Macat Disciplines

Access the greatest ideas and thinkers across entire disciplines, including

MAN AND THE ENVIRONMENT

The Brundtland Report's, *Our Common Future*
Rachel Carson's, *Silent Spring*
James Lovelock's, *Gaia: A New Look at Life on Earth*
Mathis Wackernagel & William Rees's, *Our Ecological Footprint*

Macat analyses are available from all good bookshops and libraries.

Access hundreds of analyses through one, multimedia tool.
Join free for one month **library.macat.com**

Macat Pairs

Analyse historical and modern issues from opposite sides of an argument. Pairs include:

ARE WE FUNDAMENTALLY GOOD - OR BAD?

Steven Pinker's
The Better Angels of Our Nature

Stephen Pinker's gloriously optimistic 2011 book argues that, despite humanity's biological tendency toward violence, we are, in fact, less violent today than ever before. To prove his case, Pinker lays out pages of detailed statistical evidence. For him, much of the credit for the decline goes to the eighteenth-century Enlightenment movement, whose ideas of liberty, tolerance, and respect for the value of human life filtered down through society and affected how people thought. That psychological change led to behavioral change—and overall we became more peaceful. Critics countered that humanity could never overcome the biological urge toward violence; others argued that Pinker's statistics were flawed.

Philip Zimbardo's
The Lucifer Effect

Some psychologists believe those who commit cruelty are innately evil. Zimbardo disagrees. In *The Lucifer Effect*, he argues that sometimes good people do evil things simply because of the situations they find themselves in, citing many historical examples to illustrate his point. Zimbardo details his 1971 Stanford prison experiment, where ordinary volunteers playing guards in a mock prison rapidly became abusive. But he also describes the tortures committed by US army personnel in Iraq's Abu Ghraib prison in 2003—and how he himself testified in defence of one of those guards. committed by US army personnel in Iraq's Abu Ghraib prison in 2003—and how he himself testified in defence of one of those guards.

Macat analyses are available from all good bookshops and libraries.

Access hundreds of analyses through one, multimedia tool.

Macat Pairs

Analyse historical and modern issues from opposite sides of an argument. Pairs include:

HOW WE RELATE TO EACH OTHER AND SOCIETY

Jean-Jacques Rousseau's
The Social Contract

Rousseau's famous work sets out the radical concept of the 'social contract': a give-and-take relationship between individual freedom and social order.

If people are free to do as they like, governed only by their own sense of justice, they are also vulnerable to chaos and violence. To avoid this, Rousseau proposes, they should agree to give up some freedom to benefit from the protection of social and political organization. But this deal is only just if societies are led by the collective needs and desires of the people, and able to control the private interests of individuals. For Rousseau, the only legitimate form of government is rule by the people.

Robert D. Putnam's
Bowling Alone

In *Bowling Alone*, Robert Putnam argues that Americans have become disconnected from one another and from the institutions of their common life, and investigates the consequences of this change.

Looking at a range of indicators, from membership in formal organizations to the number of invitations being extended to informal dinner parties, Putnam demonstrates that Americans are interacting less and creating less "social capital" – with potentially disastrous implications for their society.

It would be difficult to overstate the impact of *Bowling Alone*, one of the most frequently cited social science publications of the last half-century.

Macat analyses are available from all good bookshops and libraries.

Access hundreds of analyses through one, multimedia tool.
Join free for one month **library.macat.com**